PURCHASING IN THE INDUSTRIAL, INSTITUTIONAL, GOVERNMENTAL, AND RETAIL SECTORS: A COMPARATIVE STUDY

by

Michael G. Kolchin, Ph.D., C.P.M.

College of Business and Economics

Lehigh University

ACKNOWLEDGMENTS •

THE CENTER FOR ADVANCED PURCHASING STUDIES would like to thank more than 1,300 purchasing professionals who responded to the survey used to collect data for this study, as well as the individuals who were interviewed to provide supporting information.

For their assistance in preparation of the manuscript at CAPS, thanks go to Carol Ketchum, Administrative Assistant; Linda Stanley, Graduate Research Associate; Wendy Richards, Secretary; Michelle Gomez, Secretary; and Richard Boyle, Assistant Director.

Finally, five purchasing executives/academics served on the ad hoc industry/research advisory committee for this study. Their comments and review of the draft manuscript helped strengthen the analysis of the data. Special thanks are due to:

- Wayne Wittig, Office of Federal Procurement Policy
- Harry R. Page, The George Washington University
- Joel Wise, (formerly) Associated Dry Goods Corporation
- Gerald F. Evans, University of Arizona
- Therese M. Maskulka, Lehigh University

Of course, complete responsibility for the final study rests with the author of this report.

ISBN: 0-945968-06-X

LCCN: 90-61278

CONTENTS •

TABLES, EXHIBITS, AND APPENDIX •

PREFACE •

This comparative study of the buying practices and profiles of purchasing professionals in the various sectors of the economy was undertaken to identify the similarities and differences among them. While there are a number of substantial differences, there are also enough similarities to suggest that a common body of purchasing knowledge exists. In short, "good buying is good buying," regardless of the sector.

The study that follows identifies these similarities and differences and highlights issues that are of concern to all purchasing professionals whether they be in the industrial, institutional, governmental, or retailing sectors.

SUMMARY AND IMPLICATIONS OF THE STUDY •

The results of this extensive study of purchasing in the industrial, institutional, governmental, and retailing sectors clearly establish a number of similarities in both the jobs and the people who make up the purchasing profession across the various sectors. At the same time, there are some significant differences. Most especially, there is a substantial difference in pay levels between purchasing professionals in the private and public sectors. And, as expected, there were significant differences in the degree of formalization in the purchasing function between the public and private sectors, with the public sector being much more heavily formalized. While it is difficult to draw any specific conclusions from the data reported in this study of purchasing professionals in the various sectors, there are a number of interesting patterns that can be highlighted. Perhaps one of the most striking similarities is the predominance of men in purchasing positions. For the overall study, it would appear that only 25 percent of the sample were women. A future study of this sort might find the number of women in purchasing increasing at a rapid rate. This conclusion is supported by the findings of the 1989 NAPM Membership Profile in which the percentage of women members in the NAPM had increased from 16.9 percent in 1986 to 25.0 percent in 1989, an increase of 47.9 percent. Further, what this extensive review of the buying processes in the various sectors of the economy seems to indicate is that the goal of buyers in each of the sectors is essentially identical; that is, all buyers are interested in buying goods and services that meet the needs of their customers at the lowest total cost possible. The methods used by each sector to obtain this goal may differ somewhat, but they also share a good deal of similarity. In addition, the major concerns of buyers in all sectors are quite similar. These similarities are discussed below:

1. *Goal and Processes*—As just mentioned, the goal of all buyers is essentially the same. Goods are bought to satisfy the needs of customers of the buyer. This includes internal customers of industrial, institutional, and governmental buyers and the company's customers in the case of retail buyers. While this may seem to be a major difference between the purchase of goods for resale and those that are not for resale, it is interesting to note that many industrial buyers are becoming more cognizant of their final customer's needs as well.

The processes followed by each sector also demonstrate a number of similarities. In all cases, a need is identified, qualified sources are located and asked to make proposals, the "best" source is chosen and terms and conditions of a contract are negotiated, and performance of the chosen supplier is monitored for conformance to the contract. In all sectors, supplier evaluations have been developed to aid in this process.

2. *Structure*—Another similarity shown in this review of purchasing across sectors is the commonality in organizational form used to organize buying activities. In almost all cases, a combination of centralization and decentralization is used to organize these activities. The value of centralizing certain purchases has been demonstrated as a principle of good buying regardless of sector. At the same time, flexibility dictates the need for some level of decentralization when economies of scale are not obtained through corporate contracts.

3. *Reliable Suppliers*—The key to good buying in all sectors discussed in this review is the ability to select, develop, and maintain reliable suppliers. With this in mind, all sectors, except the governmental sector, have sought to develop better relationships with their suppliers by looking upon them as extensions to their own company. Even in the government sector, there has been the realization that greater cooperation with suppliers will result in better purchasing.

4. *A Professional Work Force*—Another key to good buying is the development of a highly qualified and professional work force. In order to achieve such lofty goals, buyers in all sectors have turned to professional organizations in search of means by which professional purchasing people can improve themselves.

In an attempt to improve the professionalism of their members, each of these organizations has developed educational and training programs that lead to professional certification.

These results also show an increasing level of education being achieved by buyers in all sectors.

6

This is partly the result of many organizations now requiring college degrees of people they hire into entry-level positions in purchasing.

5. *Improved Purchasing Methods*—This review of purchasing across sectors has also demonstrated the pursuit of better purchasing through improved buying practices. These include:
- Value analysis
- Use of specifications
- Make-or-buy analysis
- Standardization
- Systems contracting
- Master distributors
- Information technology (e.g., EDI, FAX).

6. *Cost Containment*—In their efforts to hold the line on costs, most organizations have come to realize the importance of their purchasing departments in attaining this goal. Good buying results in lower costs. The key to achieving this goal is the early involvement of purchasing in the procurement process so as to ensure that good buying occurs. This is perhaps the most important common goal of buyers in all sectors because, with the exception of the retailing sector, many buyers are still struggling to achieve this goal of early involvement.

Obviously, there are differences between the buying process in each of the sectors, and they should not be dismissed. Examples of these include the closeness of the retail buyer to his or her final customer and the procedural detail involved in government procurement.

Additionally, each sector has its unique purchases requiring special handling. But even here, such uniqueness could be found among different industrial firms. These differences may not result so much from their being in different sectors as much as they result from different organizational purposes.

Finally, one major difference that does occur between profit and not-for-profit purchasing is the use of buying cooperatives. Clearly, one of the essentials of good buying is attainment of buying leverage. Since many not-for-profit organizations are unable to do this on their own, they bind together and group their purchases in hopes of obtaining better prices.

In any case, buying in one sector differs from that in another mostly by degree; one sector's buying process does not differ significantly from another's. What this means is that there is a common body of purchasing knowledge that is applicable to all sectors with some modification required for each particular situation. Additionally, this would suggest that each sector has experience in particular areas that it could share with other sectors. For instance, hospitals have substantial experience in the disposal of hazardous waste, and retailers have long been using bar coding for pricing and inventory control. For the development of the profession as a whole, it would seem that bringing these various groups together and improving upon the common body of purchasing knowledge is a natural extension of the current efforts of professional associations in each of these sectors.

DESIGN OF THE STUDY •

This comparative study of the buying processes in the industrial, institutional, governmental, and retailing sectors was undertaken to identify the similarities and differences among sectors and to attempt to identify a common body of purchasing knowledge that applies regardless of sector. This objective was achieved by a threefold method:

1. Data were collected from samples of the National Association of Purchasing Management (NAPM), the National Association of Educational Buyers (NAEB), and the National Institute of Governmental Purchasing (NIGP), which allowed for comparisons of personal characteristics and job characteristics of purchasing professionals in each of these organizations.

2. A review of the literature was conducted to identify similarities and differences in the buying processes in each sector. In each case, institutional, governmental, and retailing, comparisons were made with current issues and practices in industrial purchasing.

3. In-depth interviews were conducted with representatives of the institutional, governmental, and retailing sectors to supplement the information discovered in the literature review.

In addition, a number of other current studies were included to broaden the scope of this comparative study. These included studies of the federal contract management process, the hospital materials management process, and the retail buying process.

THE SAMPLE •

In order to obtain a better picture of purchasing professionals in each of the sectors, data were collected from representative groups of buyers in each of the following sectors: industrial (a sample from NAPM); institutional (a sample from the NAEB and data collected by Giunipero and Stepina from hospital material managers); governmental (a sample from the NIGP and data collected by Cook from NCMA members); retailing (data from a study reported by Kolchin and Giunipero on retail buyers). The sample sizes and response rates for each of these studies are reported below:

Sample	# Usable Responses	% Response Rate
NAPM	595	33
NAEB	414	35
NIGP	201	39
NCMA	775	64.1
Hospitals	107	18.2
Retail Buyers	36	20

In addition, profiles of the NAPM membership conducted in 1986 and 1989 were included in the comparison to determine the representativeness of the other data. And, finally, an older study conducted by Fine and Westing, conducted in 1973, was included to give a historical perspective to the more current data.

The results of the comparison of these data are included in Exhibit 1.

To supplement the data collected in the studies reported above and the review of the literature, in-depth interviews were conducted with representatives from each of the nonindustrial sectors. Interviews were conducted with:

- A representative of the Office of the Assistant Secretary for Defense (Acquisitions and Logistics);
- The Chief Purchasing Official for the State of Pennsylvania;
- The Purchases Manager for a large city;
- Retailing executives from two large department store chains.

The information collected in the interview phase of the study is included in the discussion of the buying processes in each of the nonindustrial sectors.

PURCHASING IN THE INDUSTRIAL, INSTITUTIONAL, GOVERNMENTAL, AND RETAIL SECTORS: A COMPARATIVE STUDY—INTRODUCTION •

Many of the leading textbooks in the field of purchasing and materials management suggest that there are basically two types of purchasing: (1) resale and (2) nonresale.[1] Further, these textbooks state that they intend to deal only with this latter category, most often referred to as industrial purchasing. This view may be too shortsighted since these authors are dealing with only about one-third of the purchasing population in the United States. The reason given for this lack of attention to other forms of buying is the assumption that they are quite different and, therefore, cannot be covered simultaneously. For example, Donald W. Dobler, Lamar Lee, Jr., and David N. Burt distinguish between these two categories of buyers:

Merchandise Buyer
Today's merchants ascertain what consumers want, buy it at a price to which they can add a profitable markup, and sell it to the customer at a satisfactory level of quality and service.

Industrial Buyer
The role of the industrial buyer is more complex in that their actions must be more closely integrated with other functions of the firm.[2]

In today's world, however, it may well be that the merchandise buyer must also act in closer coordination with other activities of his or her store. In short, the differences between the industrial buyer and the merchandise buyer may be more perceptual than real. Moreover, since there are more than 200,000 professionals involved in merchandise buying, it would seem an oversight not to include them in a comparative study of buying processes.

In addition, there are many other purchasing professionals who buy for institutions, government agencies, and service organizations. As a result, by addressing only the industrial buying segment, Dobler, Lee, and Burt are dealing with only about one-third of the purchasing population in the United States.

Consider the following Bureau of Labor Statistics (BLS) estimates:

- In 1984, BLS estimated that there were a total of 189,000 purchasing agents in the United States.
- Of these, only 88,000 were in the durable and nondurable manufacturing sectors.
- 31,200 purchasing agents were in the federal, state, and local sectors.
- The rest of the purchasing agents were in the service and institutional sectors (e.g., hospitals, universities, architectural and engineering design firms).
- In addition, BLS estimated that there were 229,000 retail/wholesale buyers in 1984.[3]

These estimates would suggest that there were more than 400,000 individuals involved in buying in the United States in 1984 and, according to the BLS estimates, only 88,000 of these were engaged in industrial purchasing.

Later figures provided by the BLS estimated that, in addition to the previous estimates of the number of purchasing agents and retail/wholesale buyers, there were 230,000 individuals described as purchasing managers.[4] These figures included personnel involved in buying both for resale and nonresale. Previous estimates make it reasonable to assume that at least half of these managers were engaged in something other than industrial purchasing. These same data also indicated that, by 1986, the estimated number of purchasing agents had dropped from 189,000 to 188,000, and the number of retail/wholesale buyers had dropped from 229,000 to 192,000. The possible reasons for the 16-percent drop in the retail/wholesale category include the recent spate of consolidation of firms in this industry as well as the increasing use of new information systems.

None of the BLS estimates includes uniformed personnel of the armed forces involved in procurement. Estimates for these personnel range from the figure of 3,000 developed by the Department of Defense to the figure of 12,000 developed by Harry

R. Page, a noted expert in the public purchasing field.[5] In fact, Page has developed more detailed estimates for each of the sectors of the economy, which differ somewhat from the BLS estimates stated earlier. His estimates and projections for the future are:

Sector	1986	1995	2000
Manufacturing	185,000	190,000	192,000
Services	105,000	110,000	115,000
Federal Government	70,000	80,000	80,000
State and Local Government	55,000	60,000	63,000
Subtotals	415,000	440,000	450,000
Wholesale and Retail Buyers	192,000	204,000	210,000
Totals	607,000	644,000	660,000

While there are some discrepancies between these figures and those of the BLS, there seems to be general agreement that approximately 600,000 individuals are involved in the purchasing profession in the United States and that less than a third of them are in the industrial sector. However, most of the literature in the purchasing field deals with industrial purchasing. The goal of this report is to begin to fill this gap by examining purchasing personnel and processes involved in other sectors and comparing them to industrial purchasing personnel and processes.

PERSONAL AND JOB CHARACTERISTICS OF PURCHASING PROFESSIONALS •

PERSONAL CHARACTERISTICS

As a first step in attempting to fill this void, data were collected from various sources concerning demographic variables of purchasing professionals in the representative samples from each sector. Examples of the demographic data collected include: age, sex, education, purchasing experience, titles, annual purchasing responsibilities in dollars, whether respondents are certified, and salaries. This information allows for a comparison of the personal profiles of purchasing professionals in each of the sectors.

Some of these data were collected specifically for this report, while the rest of the data reported in Exhibit 1 were obtained from other studies of purchasers in different sectors. Because each of the surveys used to collect these data were constructed somewhat differently, exact comparisons are not possible; however, there are enough similarities in each instrument so that trends can be identified. Additionally, the studies were conducted in different years, which further limits the generalizations that may be made about the data.

The demographic data collected specifically for this study were obtained as a part of a larger study by the author that investigated the role of structure in the performance of purchasers in the industrial, institutional, and governmental sectors. These data were collected during the summer of 1986 through a mail survey sent to selected samples from the National Association of Purchasing Management (NAPM), the National Association of Educational Buyers (NAEB), and the National Institute of Governmental Purchasing (NIGP). These groups represent industrial, institutional, and governmental purchasers, respectively. The response rates for each of these samples are:

Sample	# Surveys Sent	# Usable Responses	% Response Rate
NAPM	1,784	595	33
NAEB	1,171	414	35
NIGP	515	201	39
Total	**3,470**	**1,210**	**35**

The preceding data are listed in Exhibit 1 under the columns titled Kolchin 1986.

To put these data in perspective, Exhibit 1 also reports the data collected by the NAPM describing the profile of their membership.[6] The data reported there are listed under the heading of NAPM 1986 Profile. The 386 responses reported in the NAPM 1986 data represent a 38.6-percent response rate.

The data listed in Exhibit 1 under Cook 1987 are data collected from a sample of members of the National Contract Management Association (NCMA). These data were collected by Curtis R. Cook as part of a larger study investigating decision-making processes used by personnel involved in federal contract management.[7] The 775 responses reported in the Cook data represent a 64.1-percent response rate.

The Larry C. Giunipero and Lee Stepina 1985 study reports data collected from 107 hospital materials managers in the southeastern part of the United States.[8] The response rate for this study was 18.2 percent.

The retailing study by Michael G. Kolchin and Larry C. Giunipero 1987 reports data collected in 1982 at Florida State University.[9] These data represent a very small sample of 36 merchandise buyers from throughout the United States. The response rate for this sample of merchandise buyers was only 20 percent.

The 1989 NAPM Membership Profile is also included in Exhibit 1 in order to look at more recent trends among members of the NAPM.[10] The data included in Exhibit 1 were collected from 446 NAPM members. This study had a 36.8-percent response rate.

Finally, Exhibit 1 also includes data from an older study conducted by I.V. Fine and J.H. Westing in 1973.[11] This study reports the responses of 214 purchasing personnel in both the public and private sectors. These two groups are listed as industrial and public in Exhibit 1. The overall response rate for the Fine and Westing study was 48 percent, with a slightly higher rate for the public sector. The authors of this study note that the public group includes governmental agencies and non-profit organizations. The Fine and Westing data are included in this report to give a historical perspective to the more current data included in Exhibit 1.

The comparisons from these various studies will be drawn as each study is discussed.

EXHIBIT 1

PERSONAL CHARACTERISTICS OF PURCHASING PROFESSIONALS ACROSS SECTORS

	Kolchin (1986) NAPM N=595	Kolchin (1986) NAEB N=414	Kolchin (1986) NIGP N=201	NAPM (1986) Profile N=386	Cook (1987) NCMA N=775	Giunipero & Stepina (1985) Hospitals N=107	Kolchin & Giunipero (1987) Retailers N=36	NAPM (1989) Profile N=446	Fine & Westing (1973) Industrial N=131	Fine & Westing (1973) Public N=83
Age										
20-29	5.8%	2.7%	4.5%	5.7%	8.2%	N/A	N/A	7.9%	N/A	N/A
30-39	41.8	33.2	28.6	33.2	26.8	N/A	N/A	32.7	N/A	N/A
40-49	27.6	27.2	33.2	31.9	38.8	N/A	N/A	38.8	N/A	N/A
50-over	24.8	36.9	33.7	28.3	26.2	N/A	N/A	17.6	N/A	N/A
% Female	16.9%	27.2%	16.7%	16.0%	30.1%	N/A	N/A	25.0%	N/A	N/A
Education										
High School	6.0%	5.5%	6.6%	8.8%	2.9%	32.7%	34.3%	7.4%	14.5%	14.5%
Some College	29.6	28.5	37.1	27.2	16.1	15.9	20.0	30.5	35.1	38.5
Bachelor's	50.3	50.0	37.6	47.7	42.2	38.3	45.7	51.0	(50.4)[f]	(47.0)[g]
Graduate	14.1	16.0	18.8	15.5	38.8	13.1	0.0	11.1		
Purchasing Experience (Years)	12.8	14.4	15.7	7.9*	12.2	5.2	11.3	12.7*	11.6	11.4
Title										
Vice President	3.9%	1.2%	0.5%	(16.8%)[a]	N/A	0.0%	13.9%	(15.0%)[e]	N/A	N/A
Director	15.3	57.9	41.5		N/A	17.0	5.5 (GMM)[c]		N/A	N/A
Manager	40.8	18.4	11.5	37.8	N/A	60.4	30.6(DMM)[d]	36.2	N/A	N/A
Purchasing Agent	16.0	11.9	38.5	18.7	N/A	7.5		20.6	N/A	N/A
Senior Buyer	13.6	9.2	5.5	(19.9)[b]	N/A	2.8		8.4	N/A	N/A
Buyer	10.3	1.5	2.5		N/A	2.8	50.0	12.7	N/A	N/A
Annual Purchases ($ million)	39.3	14.9	44.1	36.8*	N/A	N/A	30.1	49.6*	N/A	N/A
Certified	31.6%	27.2%	32.0%	27.0%	25.8%	17.0%	N/A	33.3%	N/A	N/A
Salaries										
$20,000 & under	5.5%	12.2%	4.6%	3.9%	N/A	23.3%	8.8%	4.6%	76.3%	60.2%
$21,000-$30,000	28.7	31.2	36.0	26.7	N/A	46.6	35.4	19.6	23.7	39.8
$31,000-$40,000	28.7	33.2	35.0	30.1	N/A	21.3	55.9	30.1		
$41,000-$50,000	17.2	17.6	17.8	18.7	N/A	6.8		20.8		
$51,000 & over	20.1	5.9	6.6	18.5	N/A	1.9		24.6		

* These figures were collected on estimated averages.
a Figure is a total percentage for Vice President and Director.
b Figure is a total percentage for Senior Buyer and Buyer.
c General Merchandise Manager

d Divisional Merchandise Manager
e Figure is a total percentage for Vice President and Director.
f Figure is a total percentage for Bachelor's and Graduate.
g Figure is a total percentage for Bachelor's and Graduate.

13

The Comparative Study

For this comparative study, the author collected data from representative samples of three major professional purchasing organizations: the National Association of Purchasing Management (NAPM); the National Association of Educational Buyers (NAEB); and the National Institute of Governmental Purchasing (NIGP). These three samples represent industrial, institutional, and governmental buyers, respectively. It would appear that these data are representative of the purchasing population, because they compare very closely to the data collected for the NAPM 1986 Membership Profile. One area where this is not true is in the area of purchasing experience. The 1986 NAPM data show substantially fewer years of purchasing experience; however, the discrepancy is misleading because the data for the two studies were collected in a very different manner. The comparative study gave the exact years of purchasing experience; the NAPM study segmented the years of experience into ranges. The figure listed in Exhibit 1 under NAPM 1986 Profile for years of purchasing experience is an estimate using the percentages in each bracket and multiplying them by the midpoints of these brackets.

The data listed under Kolchin 1986 in Exhibit 1 make possible a number of observations. It would appear that, for this sample of purchasing professionals, respondents from the institutional (NAEB) and the governmental (NIGP) groups are, on average, older and paid less than their industrial counterparts. However, all three samples are comparable in terms of educational background, years of purchasing experience, and whether the purchasers are certified. In addition, all three samples are heavily overrepresented by males; however, the institutional (NAEB) sample is less so than either the industrial (NAPM) or governmental (NIGP) samples. There are also dramatic differences in annual purchases by institutional buyers (NAEB) and the other two samples. It should be pointed out, however, that the comparison between the industrial (NAPM) and the governmental (NIGP) samples in this category is somewhat misleading. The NIGP figures probably represent total department purchases, whereas the NAPM figures represent the purchases of a single buyer who purchases a single class of commodities. This observation is made on the basis of the high proportion of purchasing directors in the institutional (NAEB) and governmental (NIGP) samples. Interestingly, comparing titles across the three samples shows that the title of purchasing agent is still prevalent in the public sector but not in the private sector.

Also, as noted earlier, the data from the Fine and Westing study have been included in Exhibit 1 to give historical perspective to the current study. Interestingly, Fine and Westing's study differed significantly from the comparative study: 39.8 percent of the public purchasing respondents in their study made $20,000 or more a year, while only 23.7 percent of the industrial respondents earned this amount. The comparative study clearly differed: 94.5 percent of the industrial sample made more than $20,000 a year, and 20.1 percent of the same sample made more than $50,000 a year. Of course, much of the increase reported in the comparative study can be explained by the inflationary spiral of the 1970s. However, it may be more interesting that only approximately 6 percent of the public and quasi-public samples in the comparative study made more than $50,000. Why the change?

Fine and Westing claimed that their results "bear out the growing realization that civil service and public salaries finally have caught up with salaries for comparable jobs in private industry."[12] A better interpretation of their results may have been that industry had yet to recognize the importance of the purchasing function and, hence, was hesitant to pay purchasing professionals higher salaries. This conclusion seems to be borne out by the NAPM 1986 data in which industrial purchasers earn substantially higher salaries than do their public counterparts. In fact, 1.4 percent of the NAPM sample indicated that they were earning salaries of more than $100,000 a year. The increase in salary clearly signals a recognition of purchasing's importance in the NAPM 1986 study, at least in the private sector.

The Federal Contractor Study

Since the NIGP sample primarily represents purchasers at the state and local levels, and it was important to include federal procurement specialists, the data collected by Cook in his 1987 study of the decision-making process in federal contract management were included in the current study. The data reported in Exhibit 1 under the heading of NCMA were obtained from 775 members of the National Contract Management Association. The subjects in this study were drawn from both the private and public sectors. Almost 60 percent of this sample were from the private sector. The remainder of the sample were from the federal sector (37%), state and local (less than 1%), and consultants and lawyers involved in federal contracting.

Unfortunately, as noted earlier, the NCMA study is difficult to compare with other samples. However, where there are comparable data, some interesting observations can be made. For instance, the federal contracting specialists (NCMA) are closer to their industrial counterparts (NAPM) in the percentage of respondents who were age 50 and older. In both of these samples, the age 50-and-older category was substantially smaller than in either the institutional (NAEB) or the state and local government (NIGP) samples. It may well be that purchasing professionals in the NAEB and the NIGP samples came to the purchasing function later in their careers.

In the federal contractor (NCMA) sample, there are significantly more females than in either the industrial (NAPM) or the state or local (NIGP) samples. Also, the NCMA seems to represent a more educated group as indicated by the higher percentage of graduate degrees. Both in terms of purchasing experience and certification, the NCMA subjects seem to be comparable to their peers in the other samples.

The Hospital Study

In order to further expand the institutional sector of this study, it was felt that the inclusion of a sample of hospital materials managers would be useful. To this end, the study by Giunipero and Stepina of 107 hospital materials managers was included. The data from this study are listed under the Hospital heading in Exhibit 1. Again, since the specific data gathered for this study were different from that of the comparative study, it is difficult to make equivalent comparisons. However, as with the NCMA study, certain patterns are apparent. It would appear from the results of this study that hospital materials managers tend to be less educated and have a lower percentage of certified professionals than do the other samples detailed previously. The hospital materials managers are also paid less. And, as expected, the predominant title for this group was materials manager. Because the data for this study were obtained from only one region of the country, any generalization about a larger population of hospital materials managers would be hazardous at best.

The Retailing Study

As noted at the beginning of this report, no comparative study of the purchasing process would be complete without including a sample of merchandise buyers. For that reason, the study published by Kolchin and Giunipero is included here. The results of that study are listed under the Retailers heading in Exhibit 1. As noted later, there are a number of similarities in the merchandise and industrial buying processes. However, as indicated by the data reported here, there are a number of significant differences in the personal characteristics of these two types of buyers. Retail buyers in this study seem to be less educated but paid more than their counterparts in the other samples listed in Exhibit 1. The higher pay may reflect that merchandise buyers are not only buyers of merchandise but sellers as well. Their purchasing experience and dollar volume of purchases seem to be similar; however, reported volumes of merchandise bought reflect retail prices and not cost of goods sold, which could reduce these volumes by as much as one-half.

The NAPM 1986 and 1989 Membership Profiles

As indicated earlier, the NAPM Membership Profiles were included as part of this report to determine the representativeness of the data collected in the comparative study as well as to obtain a more current picture of what today's purchasing professional looks like. Including the two profiles also allows for the identification of trends in at least one sector, the industrial purchasing sector.

In the previous discussion of the Kolchin comparative study, the point was made that the NAPM sample was very similar to the data included in the NAPM 1986 Membership Profile. The typical NAPM member in the 1986 NAPM Membership Profile was as follows:

This survey indicates that the typical N.A.P.M. member is a white male who is 46 years old and who holds a bachelor's degree. He has extensive experience in purchasing, approximately 13 to 17 years, but has only been an N.A.P.M. member for six years. His title is probably purchasing manager or manager of purchasing. His employer is a manufacturer for whom he spends $6 to $10 million annually. He is responsible for all of the company's purchases and for two additional buying personnel. For this he is paid a salary of $36,000 to $38,000. His main categories of purchases are likely to be metals, electronics, or MRO supplies.[13]

The 1989 NAPM Membership Profile shows several significant changes in its typical member. Most significantly, female participation in the NAPM has increased from 16.9 percent to 25.0 percent. This percentage is now more in line with the institutional and federal government sectors in the present study. Additionally, the typical NAPM member in 1989 as compared to 1986 is somewhat younger. These two factors may explain why the salary of the typical NAPM member has remained almost constant during the three years between the studies. The 1989 Profile describes the typical NAPM member:

> According to our survey, the typical NAPM member is a 40- to 45-year old male, who holds a bachelor's degree in business. He has been a member of NAPM for about six years, and in the purchasing profession for nearly 15 years. His title is Purchasing Manager or Purchasing Agent and [he] is likely to be responsible for all purchases of the company. His employer is a manufacturer for whom he spends approximately $10 million annually and supervises two to three additional buying personnel. His purchasing department actively makes use of computers and he has access to an on-line data base. His salary is $38,600.[14]

This description of the typical NAPM member also shows the increasing use of technology in the performance of the purchasing function. It also shows a more frequent usage of the title of purchasing agent, which was mostly used in the state and local sectors of the present study. And, while the average salary of the buyer has not increased substantially since 1986, it is interesting that the $50,000-and-over category has increased from 18.5 percent to 24.6 percent during this three-year period. While some of this increase may be a function of inflation, it may be reasonably assumed that at least some portion of the professional purchasing population is recognized for its importance and is compensated for its contribution to the overall effectiveness of the firm.

The Fine and Westing Study

The Fine and Westing study has been included in Exhibit 1 to give a historical perspective to the other data included there. While the data for this study were obtained from a rather restricted sample, the responses are interesting when compared to the more current data in Exhibit 1. If Fine and Westing's data are at all representative, it would seem that purchasing professionals of today are better educated and better compensated than their counterparts of 1973. These changes have occurred even though the average experience of purchasers from 1973 onward has not changed significantly. And, as noted previously in the Fine and Westing study, public purchasers were better compensated than were their industrial counterparts. Clearly, this is not the case today. In data obtained for the comparative study, the industrial sector represented by the NAPM sample has 20.1 percent earning more than $50,000, while the state and local sector has only 6.6 percent earning $50,000 or more. As noted previously, this seems to represent the increasing recognition of the importance of purchasing in the private sector.

Summary of Personal Characteristics Data

Although it is difficult to draw any specific conclusions from the data in this report of purchasing professionals in the various sectors, there are a number of interesting patterns that can be highlighted. Perhaps one of the most striking similarities is the predominance of men in purchasing positions. For the overall study, it would appear that only 25 percent of the sample were women. A future CAPS report might find the number of women in purchasing increasing at a rapid rate. This conclusion is supported by the findings of the 1989 NAPM Membership Profile in which the percentage of women members in the NAPM had increased from 16.9 percent in 1986 to 25.0 percent in 1989, an increase of 47.9 percent. The 1989 Profile further notes that the number of "new female memberships outpaces that of males by 5 to 1."[15]

Another striking difference between sample groups in this report can be seen in the area of salaries. It is clear that the public sector's salaries are significantly behind those of industrial and retailing sectors. The NAEB and hospital salaries also lag behind those of the industrial and retailing sectors. This result is not unexpected because the hospital and educational entities are quasi-public institutions. Why does this big difference in pay exist? When the magnitude of purchases made by the public sector is considered, the salary differential may become problematic. More specifically, how can the public sector attract top-notch purchasing professionals when pay differentials are so extreme? This question is currently under investigation by the federal and state governments and will be discussed later in this report. Some would argue that the job of the public purchasing official is more routine and structured than that of industry and, therefore, does not command as high a salary. This assumption warrants some attention and is the next subject to be discussed.

JOB CHARACTERISTICS

The data for this portion of the paper are drawn from the comparative purchasing study and the federal contractor study described in the previous section. In both cases, measures were obtained to determine the degree of structure that existed in the jobs of the respondents of these studies.

The Comparative Study

In the Kolchin comparative study, measures of structure were obtained by asking respondents the following types of questions: (1) whether they felt they were behaviorally rigid; (2) how formalized their positions were—that is, the degree of rules and procedures that constrained their behavior in the performance of their jobs; (3) the amount of direction they received from their immediate supervisors in the performance of their jobs; and (4) how structured their tasks were—that is, how routine and repetitive. These dimensions of their jobs were defined as behavioral rigidity, formalization, leader direction, and task structure. The scales used to measure these dimensions were taken from the organizational theory literature and are included in the Appendix.[16] Higher scores on each of these dimensions would suggest a more highly structured job. The mean scores of the responses collected using these scales are reported in Table 1. The results are categorized by the three sectors discussed previously; that is, they are broken down into the industrial (NAPM), institutional (NAEB), and governmental (NIGP) sectors.

TABLE 1
STRUCTURE IN PURCHASING POSITIONS
(Mean Scores)

Structural Variables	NAPM	NAEB	NIGP	Possible Range
Behavioral Rigidity	21	21	21	6-42
Organizational Formalization	30	33	37	8-56
Leader Direction	25	26	26	7-49
Task Structure	27	28	28	10-50

As can be noted in Table 1, there seems to be little difference in the mean scores reported by the respondents in this study on all of the structural variables, with the exception of organizational formalization. On this dimension of the purchasing job, there is a higher degree of structure in the quasi-public (NAEB) and public (NIGP) sectors than there is in the industrial (NAPM) sector. These differences are statistically significant, which is logical because most purchasing pundits assume government purchasing positions are highly formalized. However, it is also interesting that this difference across sectors does not exist for the other structural variables. For example, task structure, which is a measure of the routineness and repetitiveness of the task, is almost identical for all three samples. Does this result suggest a similar degree of task structure in the purchasing job across sectors?

It is also interesting that the respondents in all three sectors report similar levels of behavioral rigidity. Does this suggest that similar personality types are attracted to purchasing? Also, the amount of direction given by the purchaser's immediate supervisor is almost identical in all three sectors.

These results seem to suggest that purchasing positions in the different sectors of the economy are structurally very similar. If such a conclusion were valid, however, the previous explanation of differences in pay between purchasing professionals in the private and public sectors would not be valid. However, it is not possible to draw such a conclusion on the basis of just one report, and as the differences in the organizational formalization scores indicate, there are significant constraints in public purchasing. Specifically, these constraints would include the maze of legislation that controls public purchasing.

The Federal Contractor Study

The Cook study cited previously also looked at differences in the structure of the purchasing function by comparing the amount of programmed versus non-programmed decisions and the degree of bureaucratization that existed in the jobs in his sample of NCMA members in both the public and private sectors. Programmed decisions in Cook's study were defined as routine and repetitive with well-established procedures that dictated the appropriate decision-making process. The degree of bureaucratization in his study was defined as the degree to which performance is governed by law, regulation, clerical routine, standard operating procedures, policy letters, or political factors. These factors seem very similar to the task structure and organizational formalization variables previously discussed in the comparative purchasing study. The results of the comparisons of programmed versus nonprogrammed decisions and the degree of bureaucratization in both the public and private sectors is reported in Table 2.

TABLE 2

COMPARISONS OF THE DEGREE OF
STRUCTURE IN PUBLIC AND PRIVATE
SECTOR CONTRACTING POSITIONS

Structural Variables	Federal Gov't	State & Local Gov't	Private Sector	Other
Decision Type				
Programmed	34.6%	28.6%	33.4%	35.0%
Nonprogrammed	65.4%	71.4%	66.6%	65.0%
Bureaucratization				
Not Bureaucratized	35.1%	42.9%	31.9%	45.0%
Bureaucratized	64.9%	57.1%	68.1%	55.0%

These results would suggest that the differences in the structure of the decision-making process in the private and public sectors, represented by the NCMA sample, are not so great. In particular, the private and federal contracting officers report similar levels of programmed decisions and bureaucratization in their jobs. It should be pointed out in discussing these results that the private sector, as defined here, refers to government contractors who are subject to much of the same legislation and executive orders as are federal contracting officers. Nonetheless, the similarity in

results in conjunction with the similarity in results reported already in the present study suggest a comparable level of structure in these purchasing positions.

Summary Comments Concerning Personal and Job Characteristics

These results suggest that there are a number of similarities in both the jobs and the people who make up the purchasing profession across the various sectors. At the same time, there are some significant differences. The most significant one is a substantial difference in pay levels between purchasing professionals in the private and public sectors. And, as expected, there were significant differences in the degree of formalization in the purchasing function between the public and private sectors, with the public sector more heavily formalized.

Some general comparisons of purchasing people and their jobs in each of the sectors have been made. Next, a more detailed qualitative analysis of the buying process and the concerns of purchasers in each of the sectors is developed in this comparative study.

BUYING PROCESSES AND CONCERNS OF PURCHASERS ACROSS SECTORS OF THE ECONOMY •

In order to develop a more detailed analysis of buying processes and concerns of purchasers across sectors of the economy, a literature search was undertaken to review these issues. In addition, several in-depth, personal interviews were conducted with representatives in each of the nonindustrial sectors. The results of these efforts will be reported in each sector. Each sector's findings will be compared with important issues in the industrial sector. At the end of the review that follows, an attempt is made to identify the similarities and differences among sectors and to identify a common body of purchasing concerns.

THE INSTITUTIONAL SECTOR

Since institutions are becoming a larger part of our economy, it would seem important to include this sector in a comparative study of buying processes. What is meant by institutions? For the purpose of this study, the term includes such organizations as hospitals, colleges and universities, banks and other financial institutions, and certain portions of the foodservice industry. It might be argued that these organizations could be called service organizations and, in fact, when this report was first being scoped out, the service sector was planned for inclusion. However, a definitional problem begins to arise immediately. For instance, is McDonald's part of the service sector? Most people would argue that it is, yet McDonald's is included as part of the food retailing industry in most industry comparisons. As a result of this potential confusion, a decision was made to look at service organizations as part of the institutional and retail sectors.

As a means of exploring buying processes and concerns in the institutional sector, three particular institutions will be examined: (1) hospitals; (2) foodservice operations; and (3) educational institutions. In each case, only a brief review is included, but it will be enough to give the reader a feel for the buying processes and concerns in each.

Hospitals

Health care institutions are coming under great scrutiny today because of rapidly increasing costs. Since a major portion of these costs are paid by the federal and state governments, there is significant pressure on hospitals to control costs. One area that is under particularly close scrutiny is the purchase of goods and services by hospital materials managers. Next to labor costs, materials management is the most significant cost, accounting for 20 to 30 percent of most hospitals' operating budgets, according to the American Society for Hospital Materials Management.[17] To put this into perspective, U.S. hospitals spent more than $8 billion in 1982.[18] More important, perhaps, is the rate at which these costs are rising. For example, in 1975, Dean S. Ammer, a well-respected expert in hospital materials management, estimated that the costs of purchased goods and services amounted to $7,000 per bed.[19] By 1983, Ammer estimated, these costs had risen to more than $14,000 per bed and were increasing at twice the rate of inflation.[20] However, until recently, materials management was not an area that received long-term attention by hospital administrators. Evidence of this was the low esteem with which the materials function was held and its low position in the organizational hierarchy of most hospitals.

This is all changing as the federal government is putting increasing pressure for cost containment on hospitals and other health care providers. This pressure is coming in the form of how the federal government reimburses health care providers for Medicare-covered charges. In 1982, the federal government switched from a retrospective reimbursement system of payment to a prospective payment system (PPS).[21] PPS places ceilings on reimbursement amounts by placing each individual case into one of 467 diagnoses. Each diagnosis has a single national rate of reimbursement. If a given hospital can provide service for less than this rate, then it is entitled to keep the difference. PPS is also being adopted by third-party providers, and this change is forcing a new philosophy on hospital administrators. They must now be concerned with cost containment as well as revenue generation.

This concern with cost containment has spilled over into the purchasing area because costs can be controlled there through more effective procurement practices. Again, the thrust for this effort to contain costs comes from those who provide reimbursement for patient services. Third-party providers are now insisting that hospitals follow prudent buying principles in the acquisition of goods and services. Where prudent buying practices are not followed, third-party providers may refuse payment in excess of the lowest-priced supplier unless the institution is able to justify higher costs.[22] The burden of proof lies with the hospital in demonstrating that they are, in fact, prudent buyers.[23]

Prudent buying has been described by Henning as follows:

> Prudent buying is the organization and administration of all forms of purchasing in the hospital applying uniform policies and procedures designed to assure cost-conscious purchasing practices within the meaning of sections 2102 and 2103 of the *Provider Reimbursement Manual*. Purchasing is prudent when product costs as shown on invoices and hospital costs directly related to the acquisition and use of these products—storage, distribution, processing, and disposal—are the lowest that the support of quality patient care permits.[24]

Prudent buying seems to be no different than good procurement practices. Just as industrial organizations have recognized the importance of good purchasing, now so do nonprofit institutions such as hospitals. Hospitals, like their industrial counterparts, attempt to improve their purchasing function by turning their attention to the principles of good procurement practice. For example, David S. Greisler and Sumer C. Aggarwal, in their study of hospital materials management, identified the following opportunities for savings:

- More sophisticated price negotiations
- Effective use of economically sized reorders
- Attainment of volume-based price discounts when possible
- Sizing inventories at optimal levels

- Control of inventory damage, waste, and obsolescence
- More efficient use of storage space
- More effective utilization of Hospital Shared Services-approved price lists
- Improvement in accuracy of inventory records; error rate below 5 percent
- Minimization of materials handling costs by conducting materials flow analyses
- Improvement in paperwork processing and manpower utilization by utilizing methods studies and process analyses of materials management operations
- Improved training for materials management personnel.[25]

J.H. Holmgren and W.J. Wentz also identified a number of potential cost-saving opportunities for hospital materials management in their text:

- Value analysis
- Make-or-buy analysis
- Group purchasing
- Reducing inventory
- Standardization
- Competitive bidding
- Centralization of purchasing
- A materials management orientation
- Back-up stocking by vendors
- Educating other departments on methods for reducing materials costs
- Increasing average inventory turnover
- Consignment arrangements
- Issuing instruments from one central location
- Utilizing ABC inventory systems
- Establishing criteria other than brand name for selecting equipment
- Negotiating agreements that will take account of fluctuating markets
- Educating medical staff in cost containment
- Improving maintenance agreements and maintenance of equipment to avoid rapid replacement.[26]

The primary goal of hospital materials management, according to J.J. Frommelt and J.L. Schanilec, "is to support the health care delivery system through efficient use of the hospital's limited resources. Thus, materials management considers the cost of supplies, personnel, space, and time without compromising quality."[27]

Again, all of these seem to be standard goals for any buying function and do not seem to differ between the profit and nonprofit sectors of the economy. The goal in both sectors is the most effective procurement possible while maintaining quality levels desired by the clients of the organization. Further, as in the profit sector, improved purchasing effectiveness in the nonprofit sector can be achieved by evaluating the structure, process, and people associated with the purchasing function.

In the health care organization, there has been much discussion about the structure of the purchasing function. Most of this discussion has revolved around the need to centralize the purchasing function in order to better control the cost of purchased goods and services. According to Holmgren and Wentz, more centralization is taking place in hospitals than in industry.[28] Additionally, many hospitals have long since gone to a materials management form of organization. As illustrated in the Giunipero and Stepina study cited previously, more than half of their sample held the title of materials manager and had purchasing, receiving, inventory control, distribution, materials handling, and transportation reporting to them.[29] Holmgren and Wentz suggest in their text that materials managers of larger hospitals not only had these traditional materials functions reporting to them but also had such areas as reusables and disposables, laundry, dietary, print shop, escort services, all internal and external shipping and distribution, and communications reporting to them.[30]

However, just as there has been resistance to the move toward greater centralization of the purchasing function and materials management in the industrial sector, there is a resistance to such movement in the hospital sector as well. This resistance comes as a result of questioning purchasing's technical competence in the procurement of specialized supplies and equipment, especially in areas such as pharmaceuticals, foodservice, maintenance, radiology, and other laboratory supplies and equipment. This resistance can be overcome by following the advice given by S. Randolph Hayas on how to establish centralized purchasing in hospitals. He suggests:

- Obtain full hospital administrative support.
- Sell the benefits of centralization in order to receive their cooperation.
- Establish purchasing department's credibility through a slow, yet steady, implementation process.[31]

Again, the benefits of a centralized purchasing function must be sold to the customers of purchasing if such an organization is to be established. This is true for all sectors, industrial or otherwise.

Hospitals have also sought to become more effective purchasers by evaluating the buying process itself. One of the ways to reduce the cost of purchased goods and services is to buy in larger lots. However, a major difference between the institutional and industrial sectors is that institutions can group together and enter into group purchasing agreements. According to Holmgren and Wentz, some 50 to 70 percent of the voluntary hospitals in the United States have turned to group purchasing as a means of reducing prices for purchased goods and services.[32] These group purchasing agreements have the potential for lower prices because of the increased buying power offered by the groups. However, this potential has not been reached because only about 10 percent of the average hospital's purchases are made through group purchasing programs. C.E. Housley identifies the following barriers as to why this is the case:

- Lack of commitment on the part of both purchasing and vendors
- Lack of credibility of the value of group purchasing
- Group purchasing is seen as a threat to the hospital purchasing agent
- Lack of effectiveness on the part of the directors of the group
- Vendors fear loss of profits
- Failure to share pricing information with the group
- Lack of leadership on the part of the group
- Conflicts that arise between hospitals and vendors.[33]

Another problem that renders the groups less successful than they might otherwise be is the phenomenon of dual group memberships. As noted by C.W. Moore, dual members "shop around" between the two groups, which ends up diminishing the buying leverage of both groups.[34] A last problem that makes group purchasing less than effective is lack of product standardization. In order for a group purchasing organization to be truly effective, it must be able to group together a large number of standard products. Unfortunately, there may be resistance on the part of group members to do this because of a preference for certain brands.

Despite these problems, it appears that group purchasing organizations are here to stay—if for no other reason than the pressure put on hospitals by government agencies to justify costs of materials. It is clear, however, that there is likely to be a shakeout among these group purchasing organizations with the larger ones surviving.

As in the industrial sector, hospitals are beginning to use the computer more in managing their materials functions. In addition, hospitals, like their industrial counterparts, are becoming more involved with electronic data interchange. Hospitals are also following the lead of their industrial counterparts in looking at the value of single sourcing as a means of reducing their materials costs. This latter point is seen in the development of the prime supplier contract, which is being evaluated by a number of hospitals. A prime supply contract places orders for all supply categories with one vendor.[35]

As can be seen by this brief review, there are similarities between the buying processes in hospitals and in the industrial sector. There are, obviously, some differences. For instance, the hospital materials manager does get involved in some unique purchases, such as monitors, linens, disposables and reusables, and stretchers.[36] But, even in these purchases, there are many similarities in the process. For example, evaluating linens is a classic make-or-buy problem: Should the hospital own and launder its own linens or should it use a linen rental service? In regard to disposables and reusables, hospitals probably have significantly greater experience than do their industrial counterparts, especially in the disposal of hazardous waste materials. It may well be that hospital materials managers could teach their industrial counterparts a lesson in this most critical area.

While differences exist between these two sectors, both share at least one common thread of purchasing effectiveness—the need for reliable suppliers. Holmgren and Wentz state this need very clearly:

> Responsible suppliers are an essential link in providing high quality medical care. In addition to delivering needed supplies and equipment, suppliers research products before marketing them; explain new technology; promote, distribute, and, in some cases, represent an assortment of products; transport products; visit potential customers; negotiate; hold inventory (thus partially financing the eventual sale); train personnel in product use; and provide repair and follow-up services.[37]

Hospital materials managers are recognizing the importance of a good vendor base and have developed vendor evaluation systems fairly well, allowing them to reward good vendor performance and eliminate poor vendors.[38] These practices also indicate the similarity between institutional and industrial buying processes.

Foodservice

As mentioned earlier in this review of the institutional sector purchasing, it is not clear where foodservice really fits under the categories in this report. For instance, restaurants are often considered to be part of the service sector and their employees are called service workers. But, as argued earlier, restaurants are really retailers of food products and could just as easily be included under a discussion pertaining to the retail sector. Furthermore, there are some foodservice institutions that are strictly not-for-profit organizations that clearly could be included within the institutional sector. No matter where foodservice purchasing is discussed, this segment of purchases represents a significant portion of the total goods and services purchased in our economy. As such, it warrants attention in this comparative study.

Recognition of the importance of foodservice purchasing led to the sponsoring of a study by the Center for Advanced Purchasing Studies (CAPS) on the purchasing practices of large foodservice firms.[39] This study, published in spring 1989, collected data from 61 multi-unit foodservice firms from across the United States. The findings of this study identified many similarities between industrial purchasing and purchasing for the foodservice organization.

For instance, like their industrial counterparts, foodservice organizations have purchasing organizations that are a combination of centralization and decentralization. Products such as meats, poultry, and major capital equipment are bought under a national account agreement negotiated by a corporate purchasing function, while products like dairy and produce are bought locally.

Foodservice purchasers are also heavy users of written specifications as are their industrial counterparts. In the CAPS foodservice study, the authors R. Dan Reid and Carl D. Riegel found that 62.7 percent of their sample used formal, detailed, written specifications.[40] This compares to the 82 percent reported by Dobler, Lee, and Burt of industrial purchasers who used either brand names, commercial standards, or written specifications in buying products for their firms.[41] All of these are, in essence, forms of detailed specifications.

The CAPS foodservice study also highlighted the fact that 85 percent of the foodservice purchasing organizations that participated in the study were involved, to some degree, in the strategic planning process in their respective organizations.[42] As indicated in an earlier CAPS study on purchasing organizational relationships, participation in corporate strategic planning is increasingly becoming an added responsibility of the corporate purchasing department.[43]

In addition, foodservice operations are involved in value analysis. The critical issue, however, in most value analysis studies in foodservice operations is the question of yield. Yield can be defined as the amount of usable product generated by each pound of food purchased.[44] In addition to studies pertaining to yields of various food products, foodservice operators are also concerned with issues such as functional analysis of specifications, lease-versus-buy considerations, and alternate product considerations. All of these analyses are concerned, ultimately, with the question of price versus value. Again, in this respect, buying in the foodservice sector is no different than in the industrial sector. The goal for both is the attainment of maximum value for each dollar expended.

This concern for value also extends into the area of vendor evaluation. Like their industrial counterparts, foodservice buyers have developed criteria for supplier selection based on important characteristics of what they perceive to be "good" suppliers. In the CAPS foodservice study, the characteristics deemed most important were: accurate and on-time delivery, consistent quality with reasonable prices, and a willingness to work together.[45] Again, as in the industrial sector, the "good" supplier is one who provides a combination of price, quality, and service. These characteristics would appear to be the common thread among the buying processes in all sectors of the economy.

Another commonality between the foodservice sector and industrial sector identified by the CAPS foodservice study is in the area of ethical practices. Ethics is a big issue in the economy generally and in purchasing particularly. In the CAPS foodservice study, the authors Reid and Riegel found that 61.7 percent of their sample had a company-issued code of ethics.[46] This compares to the 72 percent who had a written policy concerning ethical practices in an earlier purchasing ethical practices study sponsored by CAPS in 1988.[47] Like that ethical practices study,

the foodservice study found some disagreement as to what constitutes unethical behavior by buyers. For instance, in accepting gifts, it was the value of the gift, rather than the act of accepting the gift, that seemed important. In both the ethical practices study and the foodservice study, the acceptance of gifts up to the value of $25 seemed acceptable. Also, in both groups, the divulging of another vendor's price was seen as clearly unethical. Both of these studies seem to suggest that ethics is a generic concern to all purchasers, regardless of the sector to which they belong.

One final comparison that may be made between the foodservice sector and the industrial sector concerns the demographics of chief purchasing officers. These comparisons are made from data collected in the two studies sponsored by CAPS on the foodservice industry and the more general organizational relationships study.[48] The foodservice study found that the average age of the chief purchasing officer for the large foodservice operation was 44, while the organizational relationships study found that the average age of the chief purchasing officer was just under 50. Chief purchasing officers in the foodservice sector had an average of 11.68 years of experience with their current firm and an average of 14.77 years of purchasing experience. This compares to the more general average of 18 years experience with a current employer and six years in the present position of chief purchasing officer in the organizational relationships study. In terms of education, 41.7 percent of the respondents in the foodservice study had earned bachelor's degrees, and 13.4 percent had earned graduate degrees. These figures compare to the 55 percent of chief purchasing officers in the more general study who had earned bachelor's degrees and to the 39 percent who had earned graduate degrees. These data suggest that chief foodservice purchasing officers are generally younger than their industrial counterparts. The foodservice purchasers have slightly less education and less tenure with their companies. In addition, the majority of the chief purchasing officers in the foodservice sector are male. Only 11.5 percent of the respondents in the foodservice study were female.

While there are many similarities in the buying practices between the foodservice and industrial sectors, there are differences as well. For instance, certain characteristics of goods and services purchased take on more importance in foodservice than in industry. As an example, one major issue in the purchase of most foodstuffs is that of perishability. Shelf life is critical in any specification involving food. This concern is, perhaps, one of the reasons that produce and dairy products are bought locally. Additionally, the handling and storing of food products come under very close scrutiny by public agencies.

In other purchases, the level of vendor service becomes paramount. A good example of this is in the purchase of coffee. Not only is the coffee bought but also the equipment, and the service of that equipment. This is also the case with the purchase of sanitation supplies for the kitchen. In this case, the most critical service is the adjustment of chemicals and cleaning equipment to ensure proper cleanliness levels that meet code in the local area.

One area identified in the CAPS foodservice study that differed from the industrial sector was the size of the vendor base. More important, the trend in this area was different. While the industrial sector seems to be significantly reducing the size of its vendor base, the CAPS foodservice study indicates that just the opposite is occurring in the foodservice sector.[49] However, the conclusions may be somewhat misleading because the study neglected to discuss the role of master distributors in the foodservice industry. Foodservice organizations may use a number of vendors to supply their requirements, but most of what they actually receive comes from master distributors, such as Sysco, CPC Continental, Kraft, Sexton, Martin Brower, and Rycoff. These distributors provide a wide variety of grocery products and minimize the number of deliveries made to the individual operating unit. Since space, especially receiving space, is at a premium, this service is a necessity.

It is in this latter area where foodservice buyers may be able to add expertise to the common body of purchasing knowledge. In the recent past, industrial buyers have begun to look to third parties to take the responsibility of combining the various MRO requirements for the buyer and to purchase and distribute these items for the buyer. The value of a single order source becomes especially noticeable when warehousing space becomes scarce or pressures to reduce inventory begin to mount. In a sense, these third-party MRO suppliers are to industrial buyers what master distributors are to food buyers. So, just as the hospital materials manager can bring his or her knowledge of hazardous waste disposal to the development of a common body of purchasing knowledge, so too can the foodservice purchasing director bring the knowledge of single order sourcing.

Educational Institutions

As a final example of institutional buying, what follows is a brief review of the buying process in institutions of higher learning.

In fact, the buying process in the educational sector does not differ significantly from that in the industrial sector. What is significantly different from the industrial sector is the setting in which educational buyers find themselves. Their clients, the faculty, are considerably more resistant to using purchasing than are their counterparts in industry. Many professors feel they know what they want and that going through purchasing for their needs only slows down the process or, worse, results in the purchase of inferior products bought solely on a price basis. Yet there is increasing pressure for more effective purchasing in the educational sector as resources become scarcer and budgets become tighter. With spiraling tuitions, the public is clamoring for better cost control by educational institutions. One area where costs can be controlled is in the purchase of goods and services.

In an article reviewing how colleges and universities might contain costs, Clark L. Bernard and Douglas Beaven identified purchasing management as an area where costs might be controlled.[50] These authors state that during the 10-year period of 1974 to 1984 the costs of supplies and materials purchased by universities and colleges rose by over 120 percent.[51] Attempts to control some of these costs by switching to the use of contracted services have been largely unsuccessful because the cost for these services has doubled during the same period.[52] Bernard and Beaven suggest in their article that educational institutions can save 10 to 15 percent by following four basic good purchasing practices:

- Increasing the use of competitive bidding to achieve the best prices and best vendor support
- Coordinating closely with accounts payable to assure that payment terms for key vendors are as favorable as possible to the institution
- Promoting purchasing as a service-oriented, rather than control-oriented, department to users
- Establishing and maintaining good vendor relations so that vendors value their business with the institution and are willing to make some concessions.[53]

These same authors also cite what they call symptoms of poor purchasing management:

- Increasing number of "emergency" orders
- Low levels of competitive bidding
- Vendor complaints about slow payment
- User complaints about poor vendor support and service
- Little standardization of commonly purchased items to facilitate competitive bidding.[54]

Once again, effective purchasing principles applicable to all types of buying are being recommended. What is different in the educational sector, perhaps, is the need for purchasing to be seen as even more of a service department than it is in the industrial sector.

In the case of the educational institution, the prospective client of the purchasing department is a faculty member, research scientist, or university administrator. While each of these clients is an expert in a chosen profession, he or she has little feel for the commercial aspects of purchasing. Yet this doesn't preclude him or her from specifying a brand or entering into negotiations with a particular vendor before indicating the need to the purchasing department. Consequently, the purchasing department does not obtain the maximum value of each dollar expended for supplies, equipment, and services for the institution.

As in the industrial sector, if institutional purchasing is to be effective, it must become involved in the procurement process at an earlier stage. And, as in the industrial sector, the only way that institutional purchasing will be able to accomplish this is by providing a "service" to the academic community. This service might show academic departments how to find new products or how to stretch their shrinking budgets by more effective purchasing.

James J. Ritterskamp, Forrest L. Abbott, and Bert C. Ahrens examine the first service, providing market and product knowledge, in their text on educational institutional purchasing:

In educational institutions, the purchasing agent serves as the liaison between rapidly changing industry and the faculty member who may have become cloistered in the classroom, laboratory, or library.[55]

The second service, stretching departmental budget dollars, may be provided by demonstrating how coordinating purchases from different departments increases the buying leverage of the university. One example cited by Bernard and Beaven showed how a university saved $250,000 annually by coordinating the purchase of supplies for its five science laboratories.[56] Another way to save university dollars is through the centralization of purchases. Bernard and Beaven cited the example of Columbia University, which saved $323,000 annually by centralizing maintenance of more than 40 different types of university-owned equipment through one, on-site service company.[57]

In any case, the institutional purchasing department will only become truly effective when it is perceived as a service department and not as a department that seeks to wrest control of purchases from using departments. It must be able to convince using departments that they will be better served by central purchasing and not suffer additional paperwork and delays. Bernard and Beaven make this point succinctly: "A service-oriented purchasing manager quickly realizes that the key to cost reduction in this area is to provide excellent service to the users, who will then rely on central purchasing."[58]

Ritterskamp, Abbott, and Ahrens suggest that one way to achieve this reliance on central purchasing is by involving the faculty and others in the procurement process.[59] For instance, enlisting the help of the faculty in developing specifications or in the testing of products may help achieve this goal.

Another means available to educational institutions to increase their purchasing effectiveness, which is not available to their industrial counterparts, is the buying cooperative or group. Use of such an organization allows a university or college to increase its buying power by banding together with other institutions and negotiating attractive pricing arrangements with vendors. The buying groups used by educational institutions are either the same as, or similar to, those discussed in the previous section on hospital buying groups. What was deemed to be important to their effectiveness would apply to educational buying cooperatives as well.

The largest buying cooperative used by educational institutions of higher learning is the Educational and Institutional (E&I) Cooperative Service, Inc., which was established some 50 years ago when a small group within the National Association of Educational Buyers (NAEB) banded together to jointly purchase a few commonly used products. Since that time, E&I has evolved into a

$100-million organization that provides its membership with access to over 75 negotiated furniture, supply, and service contracts. An example is the Steelcase contract for steel office furniture and related steel products. Another example would be the national account agreement with Hertz for discounts on car rentals. Membership in E&I is open to tax-exempt institutions of higher learning and health care institutions. In fact, hospitals purchase 25 percent of their total dollar volume through E&I contracts.

In addition to the E&I cooperative, many universities belong to other cooperatives that have been established along state jurisdictions or other common characteristics. For example, the original six state universities, six municipal colleges that became state universities, two medical colleges, and several community colleges in Ohio have formed the Inter-University Council, and several large midwestern universities have banded together to contract for a number of products and services. In Arizona, Arizona State University, Northern Arizona University, and the University of Arizona have established a cooperative to purchase such items as steel office furniture, uniforms, athletic tape, and scientific instruments.

Also, in the case of state-affiliated universities, these institutions may participate in state contracts. In some states, state-affiliated institutions are mandated by law to participate in such agreements. However, in most states, such decisions to participate are left to the individual institution.

In any case, several cooperative arrangements are available to educational institutions (because of their tax-exempt status) that allow them to increase their individual buying power and, thereby, to improve their purchasing effectiveness. However, there have been a number of challenges to such arrangements by vendors who feel they have been excluded from a growing segment of business in the economy. An unsuccessful challenge was made against the Inter-University Council in Ohio; a challenge was made to the contract between the Xerox Corporation and the large midwestern universities. As with challenges regarding the status of hospitals, these challenges are likely to continue in the future because of the size of the institutional sector and its importance to the economy. In 1987, the cost of U.S. education at all levels amounted to more than $282 billion.[60] In 1986, the cost of providing health care in the United States was more than $458 billion.[61] It is estimated that the cost for purchased goods and services ranges from 20 to 30 percent.[62] The size of this sector alone will attract greater government scrutiny, as shown by the recent attention to charges of price fixing leveled at prestigious universities throughout the country.

Colleges and universities have also turned to improved purchasing practices in an attempt to control costs of supplies and services. Like their industrial counterparts, educational institutions are heavy users of systems contracts. In addition, educational institutions have turned to other purchasing productivity improvement processes in an effort to contain payroll costs in the purchasing department. Such processes include:

- Check-with-order—a process in which payment is authorized and made with the purchase order sent to the vendor
- Speed order systems—a process in which the requisition is sent directly to data entry and the purchase order is cut and sent to the vendor
- Direct order entry—a process in which the order is placed by the using department with an approved vendor.

Used properly and with the appropriate controls in place, these processes can free a buyer from time normally dedicated to routine, repetitive purchases. The University of Arizona provides an example of how extensively these processes are used by some educational institutions. There, half of all requisitions go directly to data entry for processing. The upper dollar limit on such requisitions is $500. Half of all requisitions are in the check-with-order category. These orders amount to only 3.5 percent of the total dollar volume of purchases made by the University of Arizona. Clearly, such methods reduce the paperwork and processing for many small-dollar volume requisitions. Direct order entry programs are prevalent between universities and the scientific instrument industry.

Purchasing offices in educational institutions, like many purchasing departments in industry, have a number of functions reporting to them. A listing of such functions includes: motor pool, telephone and other communication services, mailroom, print shop, travel, bookstore, foodservice, and construction. These are, of course, in addition to the traditional functions of the acquisition of all goods and services and the receiving, storing, and distributing of the purchases. One major difference between educational buyers and industrial buyers is that educational buyers may handle purchases for resale involved with the bookstore and certain foodservice operations.

Furthermore, like their industrial counterparts, educational purchasing managers are concerned about issues pertaining to the structure of the purchasing department: To whom does purchasing report and who reports to purchasing? In too many instances, purchasing is still a low-level function in the educational sector. Forward-thinking purchasing professionals are concerned with how to increase purchasing's influence as a means of helping their respective institutions to control costs.

These issues also pertain to the purchasing process. Again, progressive institutional purchasing directors are eager to see a more proactive purchasing process at their colleges or universities. They want to play a larger role in the strategic planning process. They are interested in greater use of computerization in purchasing and of EDI where possible.

And these issues pertain to people. A recent survey conducted by the University of Arizona showed that while the workload of 20 top university purchasing departments increased significantly from 1979 to 1986, the number of people assigned to these departments had not increased comparably. Requisitions during this period increased from an average 31,188 to 40,557, and purchase orders increased from an average 30,399 to 38,120. At the same time, the number of full-time equivalents assigned to the purchasing departments only increased from an average of 9.26 to 10.82.[63] While purchasing directors at these universities were able to increase the productivity of their people by using many of the processes described earlier, they feel that, with more people, they could be more effective in helping their universities contain costs.

Unfortunately, for many institutions, the resources are not available to upgrade their purchasing departments so that they can be effective cost controllers. This lack of resources brings into question whether university administrators have recognized the importance of the purchasing function.

Institutional Sector Summary

This brief summary of the institutional sector has shown that institutional purchasers follow practices similar to their counterparts in the industrial sector. As noted by Dobler, Burt, and Lee, good purchasing principles apply to all sectors: industrial, institutional, and governmental. The differences between sectors are only a matter of emphasis.[64] Perhaps the biggest difference between the industrial and institutional sector is the lack of a profit motive in the truly not-for-profit institutions. Ritterskamp, Abbott, and Ahrens sum up this thought:

> With no profit motive involved in educational procurement, purchasing indiscretions will not be so readily apparent, and the primary mission of buying efficiency will be judged on how far the tax dollar can be stretched or the budget amplified, as the case may be.[65]

What applies to the educational institution applies to other institutions as well. It is to be hoped that this brief review has demonstrated that public scrutiny, either in the form of legislation or outcry, serves the purpose of the profit motive in pushing for increased purchasing efficiency and effectiveness. This public scrutiny is the major difference between the institutional sector and the industrial sector; public scrutiny is a hallmark of the governmental sector as well.

THE GOVERNMENTAL SECTOR: BUYING IN A FISHBOWL

This governmental sector review will show that the buying practices in the governmental sector are basically no different from those in the industrial sector except in three important respects. One difference is that government agencies are spending taxpayers' money and, as a result, their procurement practices are subject to close scrutiny. In the federal sector, this need for scrutiny has resulted in more than 4,000 pieces of legislation regulating the procurement process. This leads to a much more inflexible procurement process than found in the private sector.

Another important difference is that government agencies attempt to carry out social policy through procurement. Legislation pertinent to government procurement attempts to accomplish such things as: the development of domestic and local businesses through laws like the Buy American Act and local preference laws; the development of small and disadvantaged businesses through set-asides for such businesses or awards to businesses in areas of labor surplus; and the development of minority-owned and women-owned businesses by requiring that a percentage of contracts let by the Department of Defense (DOD) go to such businesses.

The other major difference between governmental procurement and industrial procurement sectors is that government is a sovereign power. This means, basically, that government can change the rules of how it chooses to do business with its contractors. It can do this because of its size and relative buying power. In some respects, this situation occurs in the private sector when a large buyer does business with a small supplier that depends for its livelihood on the buyer. But, just as in the private sector, an abuse of this power can diminish the supplier base as more and more suppliers choose not to do business with the government.

In addition to these major differences between government and industrial procurement, one has to be impressed with the sheer volume of purchases of the governmental sector. Estimates of this size vary, but consider some of the following numbers.

Herman Holtz, in an article illustrating how big a market opportunity the government sector is, estimated the total purchases made by all levels of government—federal, state, and local—at $650 billion annually. Of this total, Holtz estimated that the federal government spent $200 billion and the rest was spent by approximately 80,000 autonomous or semiautonomous governmental units at the state and local levels. These estimates were obtained from Census Bureau figures that identified 79,913 autonomous or semiautonomous governmental units, which included 3,042 counties, 35,684 cities and towns, 15,174 local school districts, 25,962 special districts, plus the federal government and the 50 state governments.[66]

Harry R. Page, in his text on public purchasing, estimated that over 20 percent of GNP was represented by the goods and services purchased by the public sector. In fiscal year 1979, Page estimated the total amount spent by this sector was approximately $500 billion—$200 billion at the federal level and $300 billion at the state and local level. In addition to the dollars being spent, Page also pointed out the large numbers of people involved in the overall procurement process in the governmental sector. He estimated that 417,000 people were involved at the state and local levels, while 139,000 were involved at the federal level. These figures are based on 1979 fiscal year estimates.[67]

Not only is the sheer size of these figures impressive but also the rate at which they are growing. For instance, the Council of State and Local Governments reported in 1975 that expenditures in 1963 were $25.3 billion by state and local governments and

$38.9 billion by the federal government. By 1973, these figures had increased to $75.7 billion at the state and local level and $53.8 billion at the federal level.[68] Stanley Sherman reported that by 1979 the federal government's level of expenditures had risen to $94 billion. By 1983, this figure had risen to $168 billion. Sherman also reported that the 1983 amount represented 21 million contract actions by federal procurement personnel.[69] In 1987, this level had risen to more than $197 billion representing more than 22 million contract actions, according to data reported in Dobler, Burt, and Lee.[70]

These estimates of the size of government procurement activity attest to the importance of this sector in the health of the U.S. economy. For this reason, a review of the buying process used in the governmental sector is included in this comparison of buying processes across sectors. A brief review follows of the buying process at two levels: federal, and state and local. The information used to develop this section was obtained by reviewing periodicals and texts pertaining to public purchasing as well as by interviews with individuals at each of the federal, state, and municipal levels. The review basically demonstrates that, with a few major exceptions, the goals and the process used in government procurement are similar to those in the industrial sector. Again, the stated goals of both processes are the same. Both sectors are interested in obtaining maximum value for their purchasing dollars. The methods used to attain these goals are somewhat different, as highlighted below.

Federal Procurement

While there are many agencies that have purchasing responsibility within the federal government, this review will concentrate on the practices used by contracting officers in the Department of Defense (DOD). Of the approximate $200 billion spent by the federal government annually, DOD spends approximately 80 percent of this amount. In addition, DOD has been in the public eye recently because of rumored scandals within the agency.

An example of this notoriety was the cover story of the July 4, 1988 issue of *Business Week,* "The Defense Scandal."[71] In the article, accusations are thrown back and forth between federal contractors, legislators, and government personnel. The article suggests that the fallout from all of this consternation over the procurement process in the federal government is a likely increase in legislation that will further regulate an already overregulated activity. Many industry pundits are saying that this further regulation is exactly what should not be done. In fact, what is really required is the removal of many of the already existing regulations and a requirement that DOD contracting officers act more like their counterparts in industry. There is a need, these critics argue, for the Pentagon to treat their contractors in a less adversarial fashion. And there is a continuing cry for greater centralization of the defense procurement process, which would eliminate some of the red tape associated with defense contracting. These issues are similar to the ones that have been dealt with by industrial purchasers during the last several decades.

In order to obtain a better perspective of what is entailed in defense procurement, a description of the process itself, its scope, and the similarities and differences in the process from that of the industrial sector are described next.

The Federal Procurement Process—The federal procurement process as developed by the Office of Federal Procurement Policy (OFPP) is actually a 15-step process that is divided into two basic categories, preaward and postaward activities:

Preaward Activities

Step 1: Requirement Determination
Step 2: Requirement Specification
Step 3: Procurement Requests
Step 4: Procurement Planning
Step 5: Solicitation
Step 6: Evaluation
Step 7: Negotiation
Step 8: Source Selection

Step 9: Award

Postaward Activities

Step 10: Assignment
Step 11: System Compliance
Step 12: Performance Measurement
Step 13: Contract Modifications
Step 14: Payment
Step 15: Completion/Closeout.[72]

In addition to these 15 steps, the OFPP has delineated 112 activities that may be required during the procurement process. What exists, then, is a

detailed, well-defined series of activities to be carried out during the procurement process in the federal sector.

According to Page, in some larger federal organizations the responsibilities are divided among two different contracting officers.[73] The preaward activities up to and including the award of a contract fall under the duties of a Purchasing Contracting Officer (PCO), and the postaward activities are administered by an Administrative Contracting Officer (ACO). In addition, Page describes a number of purchasing related positions that are listed in the handbook, *Qualification Standards for White Collar Positions Under General Schedule*, published by the U.S. Office of Personnel Management:

- Supply program management (GS 2003)
- Inventory management (GS 2010)
- Contract and procurement (GS 1102)
- Purchasing (GS 1105)
- Quality inspection (GS 1960)
- Traffic management (GS 2130)
- Distribution facilities and storage management (GS 2030)
- Property disposal (GS 1104)
- Logistics management (GS 346).[74]

As can be seen from this description of various civil service positions involved in federal procurement, many of the functions performed by the industrial sector are performed by the government sector as well.

Sherman has simplified this rather detailed process by developing a generic procurement model that includes 10 steps:

- Needs perception
- Make-or-buy decision
- Requirement definition
- Resource allocation
- Solicitation and award
- Performance and administration
- Completion, delivery, and acceptance
- Payment and discharge
- Application and utilization
- Disposal.[75]

In Sherman's generic model of the federal procurement process, the fact that the buying process in both the governmental and the industrial sectors is basically the same can be clearly seen. But what is also evident by the brief review of the procurement process is that it is much more complex and detailed in the federal sector than in the industrial sector. In fact, as noted by Cook, the federal procurement process is too detailed and procedurally oriented. Cook suggests in his review of the process that this recognition led to the commissioning of a study of the process by the OFPP in 1979.[76] The OFPP, describing the federal procurement process, concludes:

> [It is] so complex that users of products and services often do not get what they want when they need it....The statutory base is outdated; regulations are voluminous and complex; meaningful standards of performance are lacking; flow of authority and responsibility is not clear; and there is a lack of accountability for results.... [T]he procurement process is cumbersome, costly and frustrating.[77]

As noted earlier in this discussion of the federal procurement process, the inflexibility dictated by procedural detail is one of the major differences between the federal and industrial sectors. This level of bureaucracy is discussed further in the identification of similarities and differences in the two processes, which follows the discussion of the scope of DOD procurement in the next section.

Scope of DOD Procurement—There can be no doubt about the sheer size of federal procurement as was demonstrated by the figures cited earlier in this review of the governmental sector. *Time* magazine calls the acquisition process for DOD the largest business enterprise in the world, an enterprise made up of 170,000 employees who sign some 56,000 contracts daily resulting in $170 billion in expenditures for goods and services annually.[78] Sherman refers to the federal government as "the largest single buyer of commercial products or modified commercial products."[79]

Most of the actual contracting in DOD is carried out by about 22,000 civilian and 3,000 military contracting officers spread through more than 800 buying offices around the world.[80] To put this in perspective, AT&T has some 1,700 people in the purchasing and traffic functions, which probably is one of the larger industrial purchasing organizations.

The organization of the procurement process within DOD is a combination of both centralization and decentralization. For instance, any item that is purchased for use by all branches of the military is procured by the Defense Logistics Agency (DLA), but items that are specific to a given branch are acquired by branch commands, such as the U.S. Army Material Development and Readiness Command (DARCOM) or the Navy's Ships Parts Control Center (SPCC).

The major purchases in DOD are for the research and development and acquisition of new weapon systems. Only 2 percent of the contracts let represent over 90 percent of total contract dollars awarded.[81]

An interesting side note to these facts and figures concerning the size of the federal procurement process is the predominant type of contract used by the federal government. Conventional wisdom often criticizes the federal government for its overuse of cost-plus-type contracts. Yet data provided by the Federal Procurement Data System Standard Report suggest a predilection toward the use of fixed-price contracts. The fiscal year 1983 report cited in Sherman shows that 81.2 percent of the contracts noted in the preceding paragraph were of the fixed-price type. These contracts represented 70 percent of total dollars expended.[82] Again, these figures demonstrated a similar preference for fixed-price contracts that would be found in the industrial sector as well.

Similarities and Differences—The description of the federal procurement process to this point clearly illustrates a major difference between federal and industrial sector purchasing—the sheer magnitude of purchases. To further emphasize this point, Ronald L. Schill reports that in 1980 DOD spent more than the combined net incomes of the top 130 firms in the Fortune 500.[83] But the real question is how different are the processes used by buyers.

The main difference cited by contractors who do business with the federal government is that the federal procurement process, by law, requires extensive use of formal advertising and competitive bidding. This has left the impression that the federal government buys only from the lowest bidder. Yet this is not always the case, as in the many instances in which the low bidder is deemed not capable of fulfilling the requirements of the bid. The notion of a qualified low bidder is similar in all sectors. The government, like its industrial counterparts, is interested in obtaining reliable sources of supply and reasonable prices. Sheth, Williams, and Hill answer the question, Is government purchasing really different? by noting that on a procedural level, government buying may differ, but on a conceptual level, government and industrial buying are very similar.[84] In both cases, government and industry, buyers are trying to obtain the right material, in the right amount, at the right location, at the right time, and at the right price.

The myth that government buying relies solely on the competitive bidding process is further shattered in Dobler, Lee, and Burt. The authors report that there has been greater emphasis on negotiation in government procurement and that only 12 to 16 percent of all government buyers use the formally advertised bidding process.[85] Sherman reports in his text that 65 percent of the procurement dollars awarded in 1983 were awarded on a noncompetitive basis. In fact, under the Armed Services Procurement Act (ASPA) of 1947, 17 exceptions were provided in which the government could use methods other than formally advertised, sealed bids. The Competition in Contracting Act (CICA) of 1984, while reducing the number of exceptions for noncompetitive awards, did broaden the definition of "competition" and abandoned the preference for formally advertised, sealed bidding as the means of awarding government contracts. The tenor of this particular act suggested a balance between formal advertising and negotiation in awarding business to federal contractors.[86]

In this regard, the federal government is attempting to achieve goals similar to those sought by any buyer. Dobler, Lee, and Burt state these similar goals:

- Support operations
- Buy competitively and wisely
- Keep minimum inventories
- Develop reliable sources
- Hire and train competent personnel.[87]

Jagdish N. Sheth, Robert F. Williams, and Richard M. Hill, however, argue that the two processes, government and industrial buying, are different in terms of goals as well. The federal government is also interested in achieving political and social goals through the procurement process.[88] The authors also highlight a number of other technical and procedural differences between government and industrial buying.[89]

These differences are:

1. *Size of purchase*—The average purchase made by the federal government is very large and usually very complex. This often limits the number of potential vendors capable of fulfilling contractual requirements.

2. *Legal restrictions*—The federal government is a heavy user of formally advertised, sealed bids. In addition, the federal procurement process is constrained by budgetary limitations and a strict accountability for the expenditure of funds. Also, as a result of the reliance on the formal advertising process, the government holds strictly to standardized product specifications. The best example of these standards may be the use of military specifications (Mil Specs). Most notably under the category of legal restrictions, the potential contractor to the federal government is subject to a number of statutes that dictate how business with the federal government will be conducted. Sherman has referred to these numerous pieces of legislation as "a statutory cornucopia."[90] A "brief" historical sketch of federal procurement legislation is presented in Exhibit 2. An even more detailed description of the acts to achieve social policy through the federal procurement process is contained in Sherman's text on government procurement management.[91]

Of course, since 1982 a number of important pieces of legislation and executive orders have been enacted that significantly affected the federal procurement process, including the Competition in Contracting Act (CICA) of 1984. CICA is discussed more fully in the section pertaining to federal procurement reform presented later.

In addition, ASPA (Armed Services Procurement Act) has been amended twice with DAR (Defense Acquisition Regulation) and, later, FAR (Federal Acquisition Regulation). FAR also amended the Federal Property and Administrative Services Act (FPASA) that had controlled procurement for all civilian agencies in the federal sector. As stated by the OFPP, FAR is meant to be "a single, simplified, government-wide regulation."[92]

3. *Compliance reviews*—The federal government establishes very tight specifications for products and uses the General Accounting Office as a watchdog to ensure that these standards are met. The GAO also

ensures that all proper procedures are followed in the procurement process.

4. *Solicitation of vendors*—Sheth, Williams, and Hill point out that ASPA requires the use of formal bid advertising except where specifically noted otherwise. ASPA does allow for 17 exceptions to this requirement. Under CICA, formal advertising is replaced by sealed bidding, and the number of exceptions have been reduced. However, as illustrated in Sherman's discussion on this subject, sealed bidding is to be used only when the following criteria are met:

- When there is more than one qualified supplier willing to compete for and to perform the proposed contract
- When the requirement is adequately defined, allowing bidders to bid on the procurement on an equal basis
- When sufficient time is available to allow the purchase to be accomplished through an orderly solicitation and award process
- When price can be used as an adequate basis for determining the source to be awarded the contract.[93]

Are these criteria any different from those that would be used to determine when competitive bidding is appropriate in the industrial sector? Apparently not, because they are very similar to the criteria listed in Dobler, Burt, and Lee's standard text on the subject of industrial purchasing.[94] Perhaps the major difference between these two sectors on competitive bidding is the justification process that must be used when competitive bidding is not used. Again, because of the scrutiny required of the public sector, noncompetitive actions in the federal procurement process are more difficult to justify. However, as noted earlier, they are not impossible to justify, because more than 65 percent of the awards made in 1983 were made on a noncompetitive basis.[95]

5. *Security*—Sheth, Williams, and Hill also state that all bidding or negotiation information is open to public review, except in cases involving national security. This particular element of the federal procurement process is especially nagging to many potential government contractors because they do not want information in their proposals to get out to their competitors. As a result, they decline to bid on government business, which results in a smaller group of potentially qualified suppliers.

6. *Diffusion of authority*—The federal government is a maze of agencies and departments, all of which have some buying authority. Sheth, Williams, and Hill suggest that this diffusion of buying authority often makes it difficult to isolate which agency or which contracting officer has the appropriate authority to let specific contracts.

7. *Leverage*—Sheth, Williams, and Hill also point to an interesting irony in the rigidity and procedural detail found in the federal procurement process. While it would be assumed that the government can exercise leverage in the buying-selling relationship with its contractors, this is not the case because of the insistence on compliance to rigid specifications. As long as the government contractor has followed specifications, the government procurement agency is either required to accept delivery or to provide a contract adjustment for any change required. This would be akin to what happens when a design specification is used by an industrial buyer and when a supplier is only obligated to meet what is written in the specifications. However, unlike their industrial counterparts, the government contracting officers often find themselves in situations with few or no alternatives to current suppliers. Hence, these suppliers have a position of leverage not often found in the industrial sector.

Sherman also points out another problem with rigid specifications and compliance to procedural detail. The rigid process results in several suboptimization problems by eliminating the use of commercially available products that would better fill the procurement need at more competitive pricing.[96] This failure was recognized in the enactment of CICA, which now allows greater use of functional specifications.

8. *Procedural detail*—As stated previously, in doing business, a major difference between the federal government and the private sector is the procedural detail involved. In fact, Sheth, Williams, and Hill claim that the most frequent complaint registered when doing business with the federal government is the amount of paperwork involved. Just as irritating is the complexity of forms involved and the confusion created by this jungle of paperwork. The insistence on procedural detail results in increased costs and time for the supplier interested in doing business with the federal government and, hence, higher procurement costs.

9. *Instrument of social policy*—As mentioned earlier, the federal government sees the procurement process as a means of carrying out social policy. This is clearly the case in the area of developing women-owned and minority-owned businesses. Recent legislation enacted by the government literally forces government contractors to seek out these firms as subcontractors in fulfilling the requirements of federal contracts. Examples of such legislation include Public Laws (P.L.) 95-507 enacted in 1978 and 99-661 enacted in 1986. The first provides for set-asides, percentages of federal contracts that must be placed with small and disadvantaged businesses, and the latter requires that 5 percent of contracts entered into with DOD must be placed with minority business enterprises (MBE). Sherman suggests that this acts as a restriction on a contracting officer's ability to place business in a competitive manner and, in a sense, conflicts with the overall objectives of the procurement process.[97] However, such conflicts are inevitable as the federal government attempts to balance social and economic objectives. Perhaps still unanswered, however, are the questions of what these social objectives will cost or whether they will be achieved at all.

10. *Government power*—Finally, Sheth, Williams, and Hill reiterate the point made by other authors that the federal government is a sovereign power that can dictate the terms and conditions under which it conducts business. In short, because of this power, it is very difficult to sue the government for breach of contract unless it chooses to be sued. Additionally, for many of the items the federal government buys it is a monopsonist operating in a technical monopoly.

Sheth, Williams, and Hill conclude that many of these differences in the government procurement process arise from basic differences in objectives and philosophy from those of the private sector. These differences include a higher degree of accountability, more stringent disclosure rules, and significantly greater procedural detail.[98] In short, the federal procurement process is very large, very bureaucratic, and very diffused. However, Sheth, Williams, and Hill also conclude:

> While there are indeed significant differences in the public and private sectors, there are also striking similarities between the two sectors, both in the purchasing decision process itself and in the types of purchasing decisions made.[99]

Schill also notes these similarities in his discussion of DOD procurement when he suggests that government buying is merely a subset of industrial buying.[100] And, as noted earlier in this report, the prime similarities are in the basic objectives of both processes. In essence, both governmental and industrial buyers are looking for suppliers who will provide them with quality products, good service, and reasonable prices. Such suppliers are referred to in CICA as "responsible sources," described in the following manner.

A responsible source:

- has adequate financial resources to perform the contract or the ability to obtain such resources;
- is able to comply with the required or proposed delivery or performance schedule taking into consideration all existing commercial and government business commitments;
- has a satisfactory performance record;
- has a satisfactory record of integrity and business ethics;
- has the necessary organization, experience, accounting and operational controls and

technical skills or the ability to obtain such organization, experience, controls, and skills;

• has the necessary production, construction, and technical equipment and facilities or the ability to obtain such equipment and facilities; and

• is otherwise qualified and eligible to receive an award under applicable laws and regulations.[101]

Except for the legal disclaimer at the end, these criteria seem identical to those that an industrial buyer may use in evaluating a potential supplier. Procurement success in the federal sector is a matter of effective contracting, just as buyer success is dependent on supplier success in the industrial sector.

In addition to the need for a reliable resource base, there are a number of other similarities between governmental and industrial buying. For instance, both engage in make-or-buy analyses and, in both cases, the trend in these decisions is toward buying. As in the industrial sector, there are constraints as to the amount of outsourcing that is possible. The typical make-or-buy decision in the governmental sector revolves around the issue of services. The major constraint on these decisions is the restriction placed on them by civil service regulations. This would be similar to the restrictions that the union contract places on such decisions made by industrial firms. However, as in industry, the key to such decisions is the most economical use of resources. Consider, for instance, the general guiding principle published by the Office of Management and Budget (OMB) in its Circular A-76 of 1967:

> It is the general policy of the administration that the federal government will not start or carry on any commercial activity to provide a service or product for its own use, if such product or service can be procured from private enterprise through ordinary channels.[102]

Sherman sees the issuance of this directive, as well as the ensuing legal battles over its intent, as affirmation of the principle of the least costly method of performance.[103] Again, as in the industrial sector, the make-or-buy decision is basically an economic one but one often constrained by political issues.

The government procurement sector is also greatly concerned with other basic procurement techniques, such as value analysis and cost analysis. In fact, government buyers are even more forceful in

these areas than are their industrial counterparts through their insistence on accompanying documentation demonstrating that these activities have taken place.

The government, although greatly constrained, also engages in international sourcing. The main constraint in this area of procurement is the protection of domestic industry, exemplified in such legislation as the Buy American Act of 1933. However, more recently the government has enacted legislation that has made it possible for government contracting officers to look overseas for their needs under certain conditions. Executive Order 12260 issued in 1980 and the Trade Agreement Act of 1979 both attempted to address this issue by setting the following objectives:

> To achieve equal treatment of foreign and domestic suppliers of designated nations, and to provide them equal opportunities (on a reciprocal basis in both magnitude and quality) to compete for contracts awarded by specified government entities.[104]

While there are many exceptions noted in these pieces of legislation, their very enactment suggests an effort on the part of the federal government to allow more economical procurement.

What can be seen from this brief identification of a number of similarities is that the federal government procurement process is, in fact, very much like its industrial counterpart with a few significant exceptions. One of these exceptions has to do with the source and timing of funding for government contracts. In many instances, projects are not fully funded when they are awarded. This requires much greater diligence on the part of the contracting officer to keep on top of the funding process for ongoing projects. The next section examines this and other areas of reform.

Federal Procurement Reform

Ever since there has been a federal procurement system, there have been calls for its reform, beginning with the Second Continental Congress's establishment of a Commissary General in 1775. The goals of the system in 1775 were really no different from those of today's federal procurement process, which seeks "to maximize competition, obtain fair prices and assure accountability of public officials for public transactions."[105] A review of these reform activities are included in Exhibit 2.

EXHIBIT 2

BRIEF HISTORY OF FEDERAL PROCUREMENT AND RELATED LEGISLATION

1775   Second Continental Congress established a Commissary General

1792   Second Congress passed a law providing for all purchases to be made by the Treasury Department.

1861   Congress enacted a law (Civil Sundry Appropriations Act) requiring advertising for government purchases except in matters of public exigency (established formal advertising).

3709 of the Revised Statutes

- Amended in *1910*
- Applied to the military until *1948*
- GSA until *1949*
- Other executive agencies until *1965*
- Still applies to purchases not in the executive branch.

WWI   *War Industries Board*—Relaxed or eliminated many procurement procedures (restraints returned after the war).

1926   *Air Corps Act*—Allowed the government to stimulate innovation to purchase quality aircraft (first formal recognition that sealed bids are not always appropriate).

1934   *Vinson-Trammel Act*—Imposed profit limitations on contracts for aircraft and naval vessels.

1941   *Renegotiation Law*—Allowed government to renegotiate certain contracts to eliminate excessive profits.

WWII   *War Production Board*—Eliminated the statutory requirement for formal advertising.

1947   *Armed Services Procurement Act* (ASPA)—Stated a preference for formal advertising but authorized the use of negotiations under 17 justifiable exceptions.

- Generated *Armed Services Procurement Regulation* (ASPR) (now known as Defense Acquisition Regulation {DAR})—which governs military procurement, sets limitations on the use of certain types of contracts, and underscores the importance of small business participation in government contracting.

1949   *Federal Property and Administrative Services Act*—Established a statutory basis for the procurement procedures of civilian agencies.

- Control of procurement policy conferred upon General Services Administration (GSA).

1959   *Federal Procurement Regulations*—Published by GSA, which set up civilian agency procurement policies and procedures.

- Augmented by individual agency procurement regulations.

1962   *Truth in Negotiations* (P.L. 87-653)

- Amendment to ASPA
- Strengthened safeguards and clarified procedures pertaining to negotiated procurements by defense department.
- Emphasized use of incentive-type contracts.

1970   *Cost Accounting Standards Board*—Required defense contractors to account for certain costs in a consistent manner.

- Disestablished on September 30, 1980.

Socio-Economic Goals and the Procurement Process

Davis-Bacon Act	Setting minimum wages on federal construction contracts.
Walsh-Healy Act	Upgrading wages and conditions on federal supply contracts.
Miller Act	Requiring payment bonds to protect subcontractors and material suppliers on federal construction jobs.
Copeland Act	Preventing salary kickbacks on federal construction projects.
1938	Congress ordered federal procurement of products made by workshops for the blind.

- Expanded in *1971* to include other handicapped persons.

Buy American Act	(1933) Promoted both business and labor interests by giving preference to domestic sources for federal purchases.
SBA	(1955) Small business and labor surplus areas assistance and preference programs.
FLSA	(1938) Required that federal contractors abide by minimum wage and work hours.
E.O. 11246	EEO requirements for federal contractors ($10,000+).

Plus many other pieces of legislation that may impact procurement, e.g., EPA, wage and price controls, OSHA, etc.

Reviews of Government Procurement

1894   Dockery Commission

1940s   Hoover Commissions

1969   *Commission of Government Procurement* (COGP)—Charged to study the federal procurement process and to make recommendations to improve its efficiency.

- Office of Federal Procurement Policy Act (OFPPA) *P.L. 93-400* created OFPP (OFPPA).
- Charged with carrying out COGP's recommendation.
- *P.L. 96-83*—Reauthorized OFPP.
- *P.L. 96-178*—New system should address statutes, regulations, the procurement work force, and procurement research.

1982   *Prompt Payment Act* (P.L. 97-177)—Directs that payment be made within 30 days after receipt of a proper invoice.

Source: Adapted from Appendix B, "A Brief History of Government Procurement and the Statutory Mandate for this Proposal," *Proposal for a Uniform Federal Procurement System*, OFPP, 1982.

Unfortunately, many of the attempts at reforming the system have had just the opposite effect. Legislation pertaining to the federal procurement system has evolved in a piecemeal fashion, responding to specific issues of a particular time, and resulting in a bureaucratic maze that inhibits effective procurement. Congress's reaction to most problems in federal procurement is to pass yet another law that further inhibits government contracting officers from fulfilling their mission of obtaining maximum value from tax dollars expended. As a result, there are now more than 4,000 pieces of legislation pertaining to federal procurement.

More recent calls for reform have attacked this legislative morass as unnecessary and argue for a procurement system that is more flexible, looks upon its suppliers as partners rather than adversaries, and is run by a cadre of procurement specialists who can carry out effectively the goals of purchasing. In short, these critics argue for a system that is more competitive than the current one. A good summary of this argument exists in former Secretary of Defense Caspar Weinberger's annual report to the Congress for fiscal year 1988:

A myriad of laws and regulations prevent buying in the same manner as the private sector, but we are reviewing our policies where possible to encourage more stable long-term contractual relationships with responsible sources. This in no way compromises our attempts to generate more competition and eliminate noncompetitive contracts wherever possible. Rather, it will complement our efforts to acquire more commercial and nondevelopmental products.[106]

This theme of competition is one that has been carried out through the reforms that have been proposed since the end of World War II. These reforms have addressed: the process itself, making it more like the industrial sector; the structure of the federal procurement process, making it more centralized; and the procurement work force, making it more professional. Each of these areas is reviewed next.

Process—Like the recommendations of the Commission on Government Procurement in 1972, more recent reform legislation has tried to simplify and unify the process while ensuring that the essence of the process was based on competition. The Commission on Government Procurement specifically proposed "the creation of an integrated system

for the effective management, control and operation of the federal procurement process."[107] This recommendation laid the groundwork for the establishment of the Office of Federal Procurement Policy (OFPP) and a unitary regulation covering both military and civilian procurement, titled the Federal Acquisition Regulation (FAR).

Ten years later, in 1982, the OFPP published their *Proposal for a Uniform Federal Procurement System* (UFPS), which proposed a greatly simplified procurement system that would be more responsive to the needs of the country.[108] One of the major recommendations of this proposal was that a single, simplified government regulation be issued that would make doing business with the government easier. In tracing the history of legislation pertaining to government procurement, the OFPP found that the existing patchwork of laws created the following procurement system:

The current federal procurement "system" is not an integrated system but, rather, a collection of statutes, policies, organizations and operations that are sometimes inconsistent, ineffective and uneconomical in satisfying agency mission needs in a timely manner.[109]

One specific example of the inconsistencies apparent in federal procurement legislation were the 16 found between the Armed Services Procurement Act (ASPA) and the Federal Property and Administrative Services Act (FPASA), the two main regulations governing federal procurement in the military and civilian sectors.[110] These inconsistencies resulted in the call for a uniform regulation pertaining to all government procurement.

This proposal led to Executive Order 12352, which sought to implement the recommendations proposed by the OFPP. One result was the Federal Acquisition Regulation (FAR). Page cites the goals of this regulation in his text on public purchasing:

It is the policy of the United States that the acquisition of property and services by the federal government shall be performed so as to meet the public needs at the lowest total cost, maintain the independent character of private enterprise by substituting for regulatory controls the incentives and constraints of effective competition, and encourage innovation and the application of new technology by stating public

reported that they allowed for the award of business on criteria other than price.[182] In all cases, awards are given to the lowest responsible bidder. In fact, both the federal sector and state and local sector stress the importance of responsible bidders. A responsible bidder is defined at the state and local level in the same manner as in the federal sector. The *State and Local Purchasing Digest* defines a responsible bidder as one who has demonstrated business integrity, financial capability, and the ability to perform.[183] Once again, the government sector relies on qualified suppliers to ensure purchasing effectiveness as does the industrial sector.

Like their industrial counterparts, public buyers are adopting new technology to improve the effectiveness of the purchasing function. Computers have greatly facilitated the access to cooperative purchasing for local jurisdictions. One such computer application was the development of the Supplynet system in British Columbia, which contains information on vendors and commodities and which allows for the consolidation of purchases for a large number of local entities throughout British Columbia.[184] The 1989 NIGP survey identified another area in which technology improved the efficiency of the purchasing function at the state and local level. It reported that 77 percent of the respondents now accept requests for quotations by facsimile machines (FAX), and another 18 percent accepted sealed bids by FAX. NIGP's conclusion from these results was that the FAX was the most significant productivity improvement for its members since the advent of the personal computer.[185]

An Example of Local City Purchasing

While it would appear that the state and local government sector attempt to achieve goals similar to those in the industrial sector, the state and local sector seems unable to obtain these goals because of the conflict between purchasing effectiveness and political expediency. Perhaps the best way to see this is to describe the process for a major city. Comments presented here were obtained in an interview with the former purchasing manager for a city. In order to protect the identity of this particular city, it is referred to as simply the City.

Procurement in the City—Procurement in the City is controlled by the Home Rule Charter that was enacted in the early 1950s. In short, this legislation requires that all purchases of $2,000 or more must be advertised for two weeks in local newspapers. In addition, all bid proposals for $2,000 or more require bid surety bonds.

The stated purpose of the procurement department is:

The Procurement Department is the central purchasing and materials management agency for the City. Its purpose is to purchase, store and distribute all materials, supplies and equipment as well as contract for all services provided by the City Charter.

The objectives for the procurement department are:

The principal responsibility of Procurement is to acquire the materials, supplies and services with the best quality at the lowest cost. Because both quality and cost are important, the City Charter mandates that all purchases be made through a competitive bidding process.

Organization of the Procurement Function for the City—The Procurement Department for the City is headed by the Procurement Commissioner with two Deputy Commissioners reporting to that office. The organization described in Table 3 is based on the author's construction of the organization chart, not on an existing organizational chart.

Scope of Operations—The Operations Division (not including Public Works or Capital Assets) is responsible for the purchase of $120 million annually of services, supplies and equipment, and the overall management of $125 million in supply and property inventory. This involves more than 4,000 contracts per year and more than 20,000 purchase orders.

These contracts are let on the basis of proposals received in response to bid invitations (on contracts exceeding $2,000) advertised in local newspapers. Advertised bids are of two varieties: (1) General Market Bids—which are open to all eligible bidders; and (2) Sheltered Market Bids—which are open only to members of sheltered markets (minority- and/or women-owned businesses).

TABLE 3

CITY PROCUREMENT DEPARTMENT

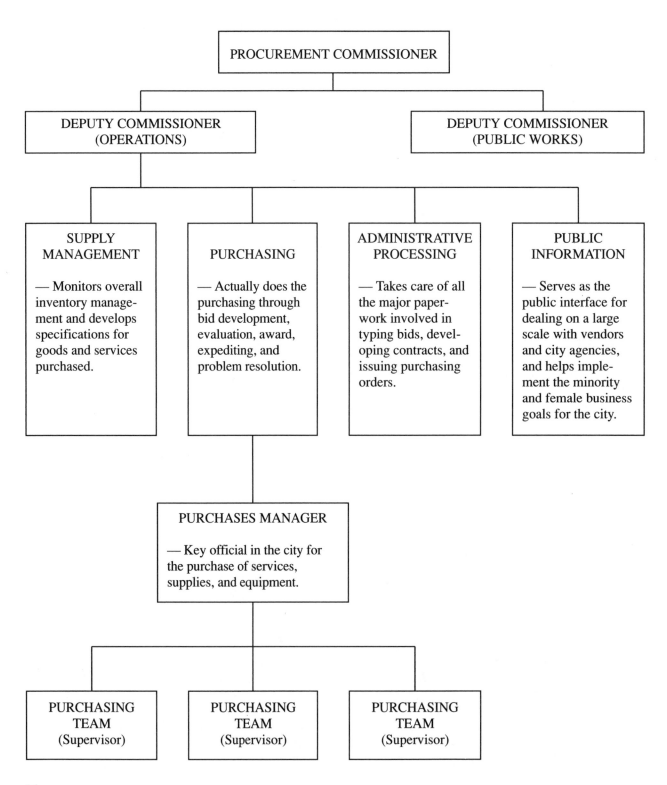

Current Problems—A few of the problems faced by the procurement department in attempting to perform its duties in an effective manner are:

Procedures. Because of the procedural detail involved in the procurement process, it takes 90 to 120 days to write a purchase order after receipt of a requisition. This problem is being addressed by the development of a purchasing/procurement system that will speed up routine and repetitive purchases.

Policy. A major policy objective of the City is to increase the participation of minority-owned and women-owned businesses. The problem is that there are not many qualified businesses in this category that are bondable. Additionally, the restriction of bids to the "sheltered" market has resulted in the development of a number of brokers—minorities or women—who bid on city business and who, when successful, turn around and buy the materials from a non-sheltered business. The result is that the City pays higher prices, and minority-owned and women-owned businesses are not helped.

Personnel. When the purchasing manager took over his current position, there were two distinct groups of employees in the Procurement Department. The older group was less educated and more apathetic. The City is in the process of trying to upgrade these positions by including education and certification requirements in the job specifications for these positions. In addition, there is a need to develop a policy manual to help new employees learn their responsibilities.

Other Problems. The payment process, because of its verification requirements, is so cumbersome that it causes problems for vendors in paying their bills. This is a particular problem for small and minority businesses.

In addition, the City imposes taxes and other restrictions on vendors who do business with the City. These restrictions are so burdensome that many vendors choose not to do business with the City. This "robs" the City of many excellent sources for its requirements.

Relationship to Other Agencies—The City can buy from state contracts, but in most cases vendors don't want to participate because of the taxes imposed by the City.

While the state has no local preference laws, it has enacted a reciprocity law: If another state has a local preference law, the first state will treat vendors from the other state in a similar manner. However, this proviso is easily circumvented by establishing a sales agency in the state.

In some areas, the City operates jointly with the school board in selecting vendors and negotiating contracts. An example would be heating-oil requirements for both entities.

Professional Development—The City is active in both the NAPM and the NIGP and pays for the Purchases Manager's dues for both these organizations. In addition, all new professional staff are required to attend the NAPM basic purchasing courses and will be required to meet certain education criteria for promotion.

Differences between City and Industrial Purchasing—Prior to assuming his current position, the Purchases Manager held a similar position for a large industrial firm. When asked to describe the differences between the two positions, he responded, "In the City, we don't engage in purchasing, we simply push paper."

In further explaining what he meant, the Purchases Manager stated:

In essence, the procurement process is dictated by procedure and allows for very little judgment by purchasing personnel. A bid request is typed, mailed out to the bidders' list, returned and opened. The award is made to the lowest bidder with only a few exceptions, such as no bid bond or a bid bond not paid properly.

The inefficiency of the process can be seen by the fact that typically 500 bid invitations are sent out and only three or four proposals are received. Vendors are not prescreened so that bid requests are often sent to unqualified bidders. This results in much wasted time and effort and added cost.

Additionally, there is no reason for salespeople to call on purchasing as the procedure dictates who will win the award. The better route for salespeople is to call on using departments and encourage users to specify their products. In many cases, specifications are simply copies of vendors' promotional data.

47

The Purchases Manager concluded his assessment of the differences between city and industrial purchasing: "While the objectives of both the industrial purchaser and the city purchasing manager are the same—obtaining a quality product in a timely manner at the least possible expenditure—the processes in both sectors differ. In industry, judgment prevails. While in city purchasing, procedure dictates."

The Purchases Manager indicated that the City may eventually adopt the Model Procurement Code (MPC) in the future. This would begin to correct a number of discrepancies between the industrial and city purchasing processes.

What this example once again demonstrates is that, while the goals of the two processes are very similar, it is much more difficult to achieve effective purchasing goals in the state and local sector, because of the constraints placed on public purchasers. What has also been highlighted in this review of state and local purchasing is that attempts are being made to improve this situation. Specifically, both NASPO and NIGP have made great strides in providing policy recommendations and training, which, if heeded, should improve much state and local purchasing. Finally, it should be pointed out that the example of city purchasing described above does not exemplify every city purchasing department. Rather, it was meant to highlight some difficulties in attempting to purchase effectively in a city environment. Just as in the industrial sector, there are good purchasing departments as well as ineffective ones.

Governmental Sector Purchasing Summary

Perhaps the basic conclusion that can be drawn from this extensive review of governmental purchasing is that the public sector has substituted legislation for managerial judgment in ensuring effective purchasing. This phenomenon has occurred because of the need for accountability and fairness in public purchasing. The question remains, however, whether legislation is a reasonable substitute for good judgment. More specifically, will legislation that specifies competitive bidding, to the exclusion of all other means of selecting suppliers, achieve the goal of optimal purchasing? Or does it prohibit the attainment of this goal? As the review of the federal sector clearly indicated, the use of competitive bidding cannot work across the board. The federal government has recognized its inadequacy by defining competition more broadly to include negotiated contracts. It seems that

the state and local sector has been slower to move in this direction, but even this sector has recognized that good purchasing is not served by the award of business strictly on the low bid. The notion of responsible bidders has clearly been accepted by public buyers at all levels, and, in this respect, they are similar to their industrial counterparts who recognize the need for qualified suppliers. Effective purchasing in the government sector is a function of successful contracting, just as it is in the private sector in which buyer success depends on supplier success.

Beyond the need for a qualified supplier base, there are similarities between public and private sector purchasing. In both sectors, purchasing is becoming more recognized for its importance to an organization. James E. Holhouser, Jr., former governor of North Carolina, states in the preface to the first edition of *State and Local Purchasing*:

> Sound purchasing operations contribute greatly to the economical and effective operation of our governments and, perhaps of even greater importance at this time in our national history, they are basic to public confidence and trust in government. Furthermore, purchasing is an important, although underutilized, resource for improved program planning and evaluation and for policy and management generally.[186]

The State and Local Purchasing Digest further emphasizes the importance of good purchasing to good government but also points to the major difference between public and private sector buying when it concludes:

> Responsible purchasing is fundamental to responsible government and, in contrast to industrial or private buying, the price of goods purchased is not the overriding indicator of performance. More important in public purchasing is how the price is obtained. Here, fairness and openness are paramount. There is no room for partiality, secretiveness or deception. Good government and good purchasing are found together.[187]

So, as noted throughout this review of buying practices in the different sectors of the economy, good buying is good buying; however, in the governmental sector, buying is performed in a fishbowl under close scrutiny by the taxpaying public.

reported that they allowed for the award of business on criteria other than price.[182] In all cases, awards are given to the lowest responsible bidder. In fact, both the federal sector and state and local sector stress the importance of responsible bidders. A responsible bidder is defined at the state and local level in the same manner as in the federal sector. The *State and Local Purchasing Digest* defines a responsible bidder as one who has demonstrated business integrity, financial capability, and the ability to perform.[183] Once again, the government sector relies on qualified suppliers to ensure purchasing effectiveness as does the industrial sector.

Like their industrial counterparts, public buyers are adopting new technology to improve the effectiveness of the purchasing function. Computers have greatly facilitated the access to cooperative purchasing for local jurisdictions. One such computer application was the development of the Supplynet system in British Columbia, which contains information on vendors and commodities and which allows for the consolidation of purchases for a large number of local entities throughout British Columbia.[184] The 1989 NIGP survey identified another area in which technology improved the efficiency of the purchasing function at the state and local level. It reported that 77 percent of the respondents now accept requests for quotations by facsimile machines (FAX), and another 18 percent accepted sealed bids by FAX. NIGP's conclusion from these results was that the FAX was the most significant productivity improvement for its members since the advent of the personal computer.[185]

An Example of Local City Purchasing

While it would appear that the state and local government sector attempt to achieve goals similar to those in the industrial sector, the state and local sector seems unable to obtain these goals because of the conflict between purchasing effectiveness and political expediency. Perhaps the best way to see this is to describe the process for a major city. Comments presented here were obtained in an interview with the former purchasing manager for a city. In order to protect the identity of this particular city, it is referred to as simply the City.

Procurement in the City—Procurement in the City is controlled by the Home Rule Charter that was enacted in the early 1950s. In short, this legislation requires that all purchases of $2,000 or more must be advertised for two weeks in local newspapers. In addition, all bid proposals for $2,000 or more require bid surety bonds.

The stated purpose of the procurement department is:

The Procurement Department is the central purchasing and materials management agency for the City. Its purpose is to purchase, store and distribute all materials, supplies and equipment as well as contract for all services provided by the City Charter.

The objectives for the procurement department are:

The principal responsibility of Procurement is to acquire the materials, supplies and services with the best quality at the lowest cost. Because both quality and cost are important, the City Charter mandates that all purchases be made through a competitive bidding process.

Organization of the Procurement Function for the City—The Procurement Department for the City is headed by the Procurement Commissioner with two Deputy Commissioners reporting to that office. The organization described in Table 3 is based on the author's construction of the organization chart, not on an existing organizational chart.

Scope of Operations—The Operations Division (not including Public Works or Capital Assets) is responsible for the purchase of $120 million annually of services, supplies and equipment, and the overall management of $125 million in supply and property inventory. This involves more than 4,000 contracts per year and more than 20,000 purchase orders.

These contracts are let on the basis of proposals received in response to bid invitations (on contracts exceeding $2,000) advertised in local newspapers. Advertised bids are of two varieties: (1) General Market Bids—which are open to all eligible bidders; and (2) Sheltered Market Bids—which are open only to members of sheltered markets (minority- and/or women-owned businesses).

TABLE 3

CITY PROCUREMENT DEPARTMENT

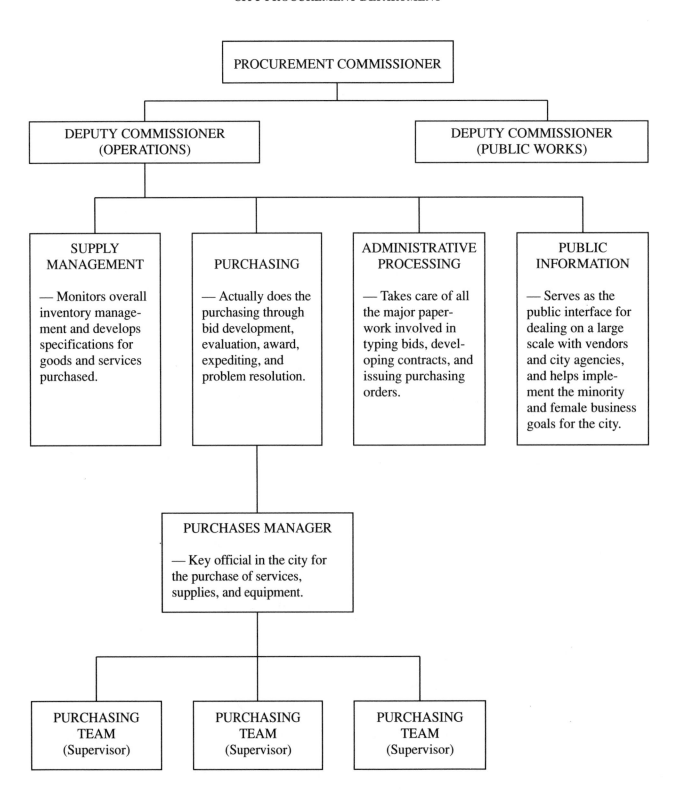

PROCUREMENT COMMISSIONER

DEPUTY COMMISSIONER (OPERATIONS)

DEPUTY COMMISSIONER (PUBLIC WORKS)

SUPPLY MANAGEMENT

— Monitors overall inventory manage-ment and develops specifications for goods and services purchased.

PURCHASING

— Actually does the purchasing through bid development, evaluation, award, expediting, and problem resolution.

ADMINISTRATIVE PROCESSING

— Takes care of all the major paper-work involved in typing bids, devel-oping contracts, and issuing purchasing orders.

PUBLIC INFORMATION

— Serves as the public interface for dealing on a large scale with vendors and city agencies, and helps imple-ment the minority and female business goals for the city.

PURCHASES MANAGER

— Key official in the city for the purchase of services, supplies, and equipment.

PURCHASING TEAM (Supervisor)

PURCHASING TEAM (Supervisor)

PURCHASING TEAM (Supervisor)

Current Problems—A few of the problems faced by the procurement department in attempting to perform its duties in an effective manner are:

Procedures. Because of the procedural detail involved in the procurement process, it takes 90 to 120 days to write a purchase order after receipt of a requisition. This problem is being addressed by the development of a purchasing/procurement system that will speed up routine and repetitive purchases.

Policy. A major policy objective of the City is to increase the participation of minority-owned and women-owned businesses. The problem is that there are not many qualified businesses in this category that are bondable. Additionally, the restriction of bids to the "sheltered" market has resulted in the development of a number of brokers—minorities or women—who bid on city business and who, when successful, turn around and buy the materials from a non-sheltered business. The result is that the City pays higher prices, and minority-owned and women-owned businesses are not helped.

Personnel. When the purchasing manager took over his current position, there were two distinct groups of employees in the Procurement Department. The older group was less educated and more apathetic. The City is in the process of trying to upgrade these positions by including education and certification requirements in the job specifications for these positions. In addition, there is a need to develop a policy manual to help new employees learn their responsibilities.

Other Problems. The payment process, because of its verification requirements, is so cumbersome that it causes problems for vendors in paying their bills. This is a particular problem for small and minority businesses.

In addition, the City imposes taxes and other restrictions on vendors who do business with the City. These restrictions are so burdensome that many vendors choose not to do business with the City. This "robs" the City of many excellent sources for its requirements.

Relationship to Other Agencies—The City can buy from state contracts, but in most cases vendors don't want to participate because of the taxes imposed by the City.

While the state has no local preference laws, it has enacted a reciprocity law: If another state has a local preference law, the first state will treat vendors from the other state in a similar manner. However, this proviso is easily circumvented by establishing a sales agency in the state.

In some areas, the City operates jointly with the school board in selecting vendors and negotiating contracts. An example would be heating-oil requirements for both entities.

Professional Development—The City is active in both the NAPM and the NIGP and pays for the Purchases Manager's dues for both these organizations. In addition, all new professional staff are required to attend the NAPM basic purchasing courses and will be required to meet certain education criteria for promotion.

Differences between City and Industrial Purchasing—Prior to assuming his current position, the Purchases Manager held a similar position for a large industrial firm. When asked to describe the differences between the two positions, he responded, "In the City, we don't engage in purchasing, we simply push paper."

In further explaining what he meant, the Purchases Manager stated:

In essence, the procurement process is dictated by procedure and allows for very little judgment by purchasing personnel. A bid request is typed, mailed out to the bidders' list, returned and opened. The award is made to the lowest bidder with only a few exceptions, such as no bid bond or a bid bond not paid properly.

The inefficiency of the process can be seen by the fact that typically 500 bid invitations are sent out and only three or four proposals are received. Vendors are not prescreened so that bid requests are often sent to unqualified bidders. This results in much wasted time and effort and added cost.

Additionally, there is no reason for salespeople to call on purchasing as the procedure dictates who will win the award. The better route for salespeople is to call on using departments and encourage users to specify their products. In many cases, specifications are simply copies of vendors' promotional data.

The Purchases Manager concluded his assessment of the differences between city and industrial purchasing: "While the objectives of both the industrial purchaser and the city purchasing manager are the same—obtaining a quality product in a timely manner at the least possible expenditure—the processes in both sectors differ. In industry, judgment prevails. While in city purchasing, procedure dictates."

The Purchases Manager indicated that the City may eventually adopt the Model Procurement Code (MPC) in the future. This would begin to correct a number of discrepancies between the industrial and city purchasing processes.

What this example once again demonstrates is that, while the goals of the two processes are very similar, it is much more difficult to achieve effective purchasing goals in the state and local sector, because of the constraints placed on public purchasers. What has also been highlighted in this review of state and local purchasing is that attempts are being made to improve this situation. Specifically, both NASPO and NIGP have made great strides in providing policy recommendations and training, which, if heeded, should improve much state and local purchasing. Finally, it should be pointed out that the example of city purchasing described above does not exemplify every city purchasing department. Rather, it was meant to highlight some difficulties in attempting to purchase effectively in a city environment. Just as in the industrial sector, there are good purchasing departments as well as ineffective ones.

Governmental Sector Purchasing Summary

Perhaps the basic conclusion that can be drawn from this extensive review of governmental purchasing is that the public sector has substituted legislation for managerial judgment in ensuring effective purchasing. This phenomenon has occurred because of the need for accountability and fairness in public purchasing. The question remains, however, whether legislation is a reasonable substitute for good judgment. More specifically, will legislation that specifies competitive bidding, to the exclusion of all other means of selecting suppliers, achieve the goal of optimal purchasing? Or does it prohibit the attainment of this goal? As the review of the federal sector clearly indicated, the use of competitive bidding cannot work across the board. The federal government has recognized its inadequacy by defining competition more broadly to include negotiated contracts. It seems that

the state and local sector has been slower to move in this direction, but even this sector has recognized that good purchasing is not served by the award of business strictly on the low bid. The notion of responsible bidders has clearly been accepted by public buyers at all levels, and, in this respect, they are similar to their industrial counterparts who recognize the need for qualified suppliers. Effective purchasing in the government sector is a function of successful contracting, just as it is in the private sector in which buyer success depends on supplier success.

Beyond the need for a qualified supplier base, there are similarities between public and private sector purchasing. In both sectors, purchasing is becoming more recognized for its importance to an organization. James E. Holhouser, Jr., former governor of North Carolina, states in the preface to the first edition of *State and Local Purchasing*:

> Sound purchasing operations contribute greatly to the economical and effective operation of our governments and, perhaps of even greater importance at this time in our national history, they are basic to public confidence and trust in government. Furthermore, purchasing is an important, although underutilized, resource for improved program planning and evaluation and for policy and management generally.[186]

The State and Local Purchasing Digest further emphasizes the importance of good purchasing to good government but also points to the major difference between public and private sector buying when it concludes:

> Responsible purchasing is fundamental to responsible government and, in contrast to industrial or private buying, the price of goods purchased is not the overriding indicator of performance. More important in public purchasing is how the price is obtained. Here, fairness and openness are paramount. There is no room for partiality, secretiveness or deception. Good government and good purchasing are found together.[187]

So, as noted throughout this review of buying practices in the different sectors of the economy, good buying is good buying; however, in the governmental sector, buying is performed in a fishbowl under close scrutiny by the taxpaying public.

THE RETAILING SECTOR

This review of the retailing sector is included because of the perception that merchandise buying is different from the buying process in the other sectors. As noted in the beginning of this report, however, to ignore this segment of buying is tantamount to eliminating the discussion about the buying process used by more than one-third the total number of U.S. purchasing professionals. The purpose of this section is to determine how merchandise buying differs from and resembles industrial buying.

The information used to make this comparison between merchandise and industrial buyers comes from a number of sources: interviews with department store executives, the survey of merchandise buyers by Kolchin and Giunipero cited previously, and a review of the literature relating to merchandise buyers.

Merchandise Buyers and Industrial Buyers: Are They Similar?

For years, students in purchasing classes have been told that there are basically two types of purchasing: purchasing for resale and purchasing for consumption or conversion. Most purchasing texts concern themselves only with this latter category, the industrial or institutional buyer. As noted earlier, the role of the merchandise buyer is described by Dobler, Burt, and Lee:

> Today's merchants determine what consumers want, buy it at a price to which they can add a profitable markup and sell it to the customer at a satisfactory level of quality and service.[188]

Dobler, Burt, and Lee further suggest that the role of the industrial buyer is more complex because their actions must be more closely integrated with other functions of the firm. In today's world the merchandise buyer must act in close coordination with other activities of his or her store. For instance, each store tries to create its own distinct image; merchandise bought must fit this image. This requires close coordination between merchandise buyers and other functions in the store such as display, sales promotion, training, receiving and marking, distribution, and the store's purchasing department. This last department is particularly important because it is responsible for ensuring that the appropriate packaging is available

for the merchandise being sold. In addition, retailing is a highly competitive industry, and buyers must consider the financial picture of the firm when they make merchandising decisions that will affect inventories and other expenses. In the past, merchandise buyers were evaluated primarily on gross margin. Today, however, their evaluation is more representative of the total profitability of their buying decisions. This requires closer control of expenses beyond those of merchandise bought. In this sense, the merchandise buyer's and the purchasing agent's goals are becoming more and more similar—to increase the profitability of the firm!

Other authors have also commented on the similarity of the two buying processes. For example, Richard Ettenson and Janet Wagner define retail buying as the decision-making process through which the retail buyer identifies, evaluates, and selects merchandise for resale to the customer. They also suggest that retail buying is really a special case of industrial buying:

- Both retail buyers and industrial buyers act as brokers for their respective customers.
- Both are affected by short-run and long-term goals.
- Both have extensive training and experience and are expected to be well-informed about their merchandise selections.[189]

This is not to say that the two roles are identical. At the International Purchasing Conference held in New York in May 1987, David F. Miller stated the major differences between the two: "In retailing, buyers not only have the responsibility for buying *finished* products but for selling them as well." In this sense, merchandise buyers are both buyer and seller, and this is how their role differs significantly from that of their industrial counterparts.

In addition to this basic difference, other goals of these two types of buyers also differ. The merchandise buyer is primarily concerned with fashion as opposed to utility. As a result, merchandise buyers must be more flexible and adaptable to a volatile marketplace. Their markets are characterized by rapid changes and short selling seasons. While strategic planning is becoming more important in the retail business, the critical planning period for the merchandise buyer is the seasonal plan.[190] This shorter planning cycle causes the merchandise buyer to buy production time and delay committing to specific sizes and colors. In this sense, while his or her industrial counterparts are making long-term commitments to their suppliers, the merchandise buyer must hold off to the last possible moment before making commitments to his or her resources.

Beyond these major differences, however, there are numerous similarities between the two roles, which a review of the merchandise buying process will illustrate.

The Merchandise Buying Process

The main similarity between merchandise buyers and industrial buyers lies in the buying process used by both groups. D. M. Lewison and M. W. DeLozier suggest that the merchandise buying process consists of six steps: identifying, surveying, contacting, evaluating, negotiating with, and buying from sources of supply.[191] This process is very similar to that described in many purchasing textbooks. For instance, Gary J. Zenz describes the purchasing process: recognition of need, description of need, selection of sources, price determination, placing the order, follow-up of the order, maintenance of records, and professional vendor relations.[192] While the process described by purchasing texts goes beyond the source selection process outlined by Lewison and DeLozier, these authors suggest that many of the other activities listed by Zenz are part of the procurement process that occurs after the order is placed with a given vendor. In their text on retailing, Lewison and DeLozier claim that the procurement process consists of the following activities: ordering and following up, receiving and checking, marking and stocking, and paying and returning. What Lewison and Delozier appear to separate into two functions, buying and procurement, Burt and other researchers call procurement.[193] In any case, it is apparent that the processes used by merchandise buyers and industrial buyers are very similar.

Another major difference between these two groups of buyers is in the impetus to recognize and describe a need. In the case of the merchandise buyer, this impetus clearly lies with his or her resources, or suppliers. This group is responsible for design, a critical factor of success for apparel retailers. The design capability of a particular supplier becomes an important evaluation factor in choosing that supplier. While design capabilities of industrial suppliers are important, they are not so critical. Most

often in the industrial arena, the buying company takes responsibility for the design of commodities purchased. In fact, as suggested by Burt, the better purchasing agents take a proactive role by getting involved in the design stage of most items bought by their companies.[194] Their early involvement in the design stage ensures that functional specifications are developed and that utility becomes the predominant goal. As was said earlier, fashion, not utility, is the key to successful merchandise buying—a significant difference between merchandise and industrial buying.

Another major difference between these two sectors is the responsibilities of buyers in each sector. As noted previously, the merchandise buyer is not only a buyer but a seller as well. Jay Diamond and Gerald Pintel indicate that the responsibilities of the merchandise buyer include:

- Merchandise selection, that is,
  — what to buy
  — how much to buy
  — from whom to buy
  — when to buy
- Advertising
- Merchandise pricing
- Management of the sales force
- Management of the department.[195]

As can be seen from this list, the buying responsibilities of the merchandise buyer are exactly the same as those of the industrial buyer; however, the merchandise buyer is responsible for a good deal more than buying. In other respects, however, the merchandise and industrial buyer are alike. For instance, Diamond and Pintel suggest that the merchandise buyer must secure the cooperation of others in the store to be successful. And, like his or her industrial counterpart, the merchandise buyer is evaluated on total cost.[196]

In many respects, retail buying is organized similarly to industrial buying as a combination of centralization and decentralization. However, except for food chains in which the buying decisions are heavily centralized, there is a great deal of autonomy at the divisional level. The reason for this, according to Diamond and Pintel, is that as chains expanded the buyer became too removed from the local market.[197] The retailing counterparts to the corporate purchasing departments in the industrial sector are the resident buying offices, which are located in major markets such as New York, Dallas, Los Angeles, and selected overseas locations.

These resident buying offices may be independent, corporate, or cooperative in nature. Diamond and Pintel give examples of each, including: Felix Lilienthal, which was a representative of several small independent department stores nationwide and is now defunct; the corporate buying offices of May Merchandising, which is involved in the buying of private labels for the May Department Store chain; and Associated Merchandising Corporation, which is a cooperative of many large department stores throughout the country.[198] This last association is akin to the buying groups and cooperatives discussed in the previous sections on institutional and governmental purchasing. The purpose of these buying offices is the same as that in any centralized purchasing organization: They desire to increase purchasing effectiveness through greater buying volume and to increase product and market knowledge gained by specialization and greater standardization.

According to the *NRMA Buyer's Manual*, buyers in most department stores are highly specialized along product lines, such as men's shirts and ties, or small kitchen electronics. Each buyer normally has responsibility for product selection, specifications, vendor selection, contract commitment, catalog copy and presentation, and acquiring product sales training materials.[199] Again, similarities exist in the responsibilities between buyers in both the retail and industrial sectors. But, again, the major difference is that merchandise buyers are also responsible for selling the products they buy.

For merchandise buyers and industrial buyers, however, the actual buying decision is similar. The merchandise buyer, like his industrial counterpart, must decide whether to buy direct from the manufacturer or from a middleman. The reasons for choosing either direct shipments from a manufacturer or store-door deliveries from a wholesaler are essentially the same in both sectors. The retailer's decision revolves around whether he or she chooses to perform the distribution function. In the case of smaller retailers, this simply may not be a choice due to space constraints. In the case of a larger chain, such as J.C. Penney, it chooses to buy direct from the manufacturer for most of its purchases, because of the sheer volume of its purchases and its extensive distribution system.

Other reasons for choosing to deal with a wholesaler include a faster response time and smaller deliveries. A recent study by Michael Levy and Michael Van Breda found that lead times from a wholesaler were substantially shorter than when buying direct. In their study, they found that the average lead time from a wholesaler was seven days while that from a manufacturer was 28 days.[200] These benefits of reduced lead times and smaller orders mean that the average inventory held by the retailer will be smaller, with a corresponding reduction in inventory carrying costs. In addition, many wholesalers in a retail distribution chain will provide marking services, which in turn allows labor savings for a retailer. Finally, the use of some wholesalers allows for consolidation of deliveries to individual stores. Because receiving space at branch stores may be minimal, this could be a significant benefit. All these reasons are similar to those used by industrial buyers in purchasing from a distributor as opposed to purchasing direct from a manufacturer.

The retail buyer must also decide whether to maintain a large vendor base to ensure innovation and competitiveness or to limit the number of vendors and increase leverage. Like their industrial counterparts, retail buyers must weigh the advantages and disadvantages of each strategy. The key to making this decision in the retailing sector, as in the other sectors discussed previously, is the need to maintain a strong, loyal vendor base that will respond to emergencies, provide innovative designs, and keep the firm competitive in a fiercely competitive industry.

The *NRMA Buyer's Manual* suggests that one way to achieve this goal is by building key resource or partner relationships. These relationships will result in greater bargaining power for the store, because the store becomes important to a few key resources.[201] The *NRMA Buyer's Manual* goes on to claim, "In a time of dynamic change in the wholesale marketplace, successful retailers are giving high priority to developing and maintaining strong relationships with their vendors."[202]

One of the ways of building these strong relationships, suggested by the *NRMA Buyer's Manual*, is to split the volume of key products among two or three key vendors.[203] This will ensure fast response to the store's needs. Additionally, concentration with fewer resources means better terms, lower buying expenses, and preferred treatment. Once again, single sourcing or sourcing with a smaller vendor base works as well for retailers as it does for industrial firms. The problems associated with a smaller vendor base are also the same in both sectors. Specifically, overdependence on a single source could result in disaster if something were to happen to that source, such as bankruptcy, fire, or strikes. The sourcing decision requires a balance between too many sources and too few sources.

Another way of looking at the size of the vendor base is the costs in dealing with too many suppliers. As suggested by Edwin Crooks, too many vendors can have a negative effect on profits by increasing costs associated with ordering, freight, and receiving. Crooks echoes the sentiment expressed earlier about the need to become important to one's vendors.[204]

One special case concerning the number of vendors was discussed in an interview with executives of the J.C. Penney chain. They indicated that the need to establish exclusive, private labels in order to compete with fashion specialty stores required Penney's to increase their vendor base, because very few vendors produce both brand and private labels.

The merchandise buyer is concerned not only with channels and size of the vendor base, but also with negotiating the best price for his or her store. This includes ensuring that the store receives all the appropriate discounts to which it is entitled and the best transportation costs available to the store. In essence, the retail buyer is interested in obtaining the lowest possible cost for the merchandise he or she buys, just like his or her industrial counterpart. In order to achieve the lowest net price for a given product, the retail buyer uses price and cost analysis based on knowledge of the market and the product. A retail buyer, in contrast to industrial buyers, must also negotiate advertising and promotional discounts.

Other procurement functions are also important to the merchandise buyer: expediting orders; ensuring that goods are received, inspected and properly marked; storing merchandise; and paying invoices. All these actions are similar to those engaged in by most industrial buyers.

Merchandise buyers, like other purchasing agents, use evaluation criteria in selecting suppliers. These criteria are a combination of price, quality, service, and delivery. However, each criterion is weighted differently. In the retailing situation, the price itself is not important, but the potential markup is critical. In addition, the return policy, as well as the markdown policy, of a particular vendor is important to a merchandise buyer. Other criteria used by merchandise buyers in choosing vendors include those stated by Arch G. Woodside: previous experience with the vendor, gross margin, strength of vendor advertising, potential sales volume, and intuition. Woodside suggests that, a previous product's sales success, a supplier's reputation, and a vendor's advertising support may be the most important criteria.[205] It is important to note here that the major goal of the merchandise buyer is to sell at the greatest profit possible, and the criteria suggested by Woodside reflect that goal. In general, merchandise buyers and industrial buyers use quite similar selection criteria.

According to Lewison and DeLozier, the general criteria merchandise buyers use in selecting vendors include merchandise criteria (quality), distribution criteria (delivery), price criteria, promotion criteria, and service criteria. All are similar to the criteria of price, quality, service, and delivery used by industrial buyers.[206]

A more complete listing of source selection criteria used by merchandise buyers can be found in the *NRMA Buyer's Manual*:

- Merchandise desirability—the right merchandise for your customer
- Bargaining position on prices and terms
- Deliveries
- Vendor distribution practices—e.g., exclusive arrangements and first offers
- Promotional aids
- Vendor's reputation for reliability.[207]

One final set of source selection criteria detailed in Diamond and Pintel demonstrate specific areas of concerns for retail buyers:

- Suitability and availability of merchandise offered
- Distribution policies that include such things as limited sales and specials
- Pricing policies including such things as price maintenance and fair trading (now illegal, which has led to an increase in private labeling)
- Promotional merchandise policies
- Shipping and inventory maintenance policies including size of orders and timeliness of deliveries
- Pricing policies including issues such as the fullness of the line versus the cost
- Profitability including potential markups, preticketing of merchandise, markdown and return policies.[208]

A specific example of source selection criteria is that used by J.C. Penney. Quality, price, and delivery are all important to Penney's buyers. When fashion items are bought, quality becomes preeminent; when commodity items are bought, price becomes important. Timing is critical in a retailing environment because a customer who does not find what he or she wants is likely to leave the store and not return. As a result, delivery reliability is crucial, and Penney's penalizes late deliveries by deducting an amount from the net price of the product.

Again, these criteria illustrate how closely intertwined the buying and selling processes are in a retailing firm. Whereas an industrial buyer purchases a commodity or component part that is converted in the production process, the retail buyer sells what he or she buys. This closeness between the two processes may be what really separates the retail buyer from his or her industrial counterpart. This difference is also reflected in the source selection criteria used by both sets of buyers.

While it does not appear that merchandise buyers have developed the sophisticated vendor evaluation schemes used by many industrial purchasing departments, some attempts have been made in this direction. Perhaps one of the more sophisticated evaluation methods for merchandise buyers is Berens' decision matrix for vendor selection.[209] However, this is not to say that retail buyers do not evaluate their resources. The two sets of vendor evaluation criteria listed below indicate what is considered to be important to the retail buyer in vendor performance.

The first are developed in Diamond and Pintel:

- Number one concern is margin
- Number of customer complaints and returns
- Accuracy of quantity shipped and billed
- Ability to meet promised delivery date
- Pricing accuracy
- Unauthorized substitutions
- Returns to vendor and reasons for returns
- Terms and allowances provided
- Compliance with shipping instructions
- Adherence to special instructions such as packaging and marking.[210]

The second set of vendor performance evaluation criteria comes from the *NRMA Retail Buyer's Manual*:

- Sales analysis—what's selling?
- Periodic examination of stocks
- Personal comments from customers and salespeople
- Customer requests noted on the selling floor
- Markup as compared to comparable merchandise

- Markdowns—why are they occurring?
- Was merchandise received in time for peak selling period?
- Were alteration, refinishing, or repair costs excessive?
- Were credits excessive?—Why? Customer complaints?[211]

Like Diamond and Pintel, the *NRMA Buyer's Manual* emphasizes that realized gross margin is the critical criterion in evaluating vendor performance.[212] While this emphasis might not be so great in the industrial sector, it is nonetheless there. In a proactive procurement environment, the industrial buyer, working with his or her marketing colleagues would know how the purchases affect the firm's ability to compete in the marketplace. Additionally, more and more purchasing departments are being evaluated on the basis of the cost of poor quality. A primary measure in this kind of evaluation is feedback from customers in the form of complaints, returns, and field warranty expense. While the industrial buyer is not so close to the final customer as is the retail buyer, he or she is being forced to ensure that a purchase satisfies the firm's customers' needs. The industrial buyer is becoming more familiar with the final customer of the firm.

It is also clear that retailers and their industrial counterparts are equally concerned with developing minority business enterprises (MBEs). A good example of the effort being made by retailers in this area is illustrated by J.C. Penney's minority business base. In 1987, J.C. Penney had placed more than $250 million of business with MBEs. Not only does J.C. Penney place business with MBEs, but it also helps build and support such enterprises. It is very active with the Minority Business Development Council (MBDC) and has contributed millions of dollars to the MBDC fund, which lends up to $250,000 to MBEs, who are required to pay the fund back at prime rates. The success of J.C. Penney in this area can be measured by the success of its MBE suppliers. One such supplier now receives more than $62 million annually from doing business with Penney's.

What this brief review of the merchandise buying process indicates is that there is good support for the premise that the jobs of the merchandise buyer and industrial buyer are similar enough to warrant inclusion in this report of comparative buying processes. The next section, which discusses a survey of a small sample of merchandise buyers, further supports the similarity.

A Survey of Merchandise Buyers

The survey of merchandise buyers discussed next is based on the responses to questionnaires sent out as part of a class project at Florida State University. Although there are a number of problems with the instrument itself, the results do provide some interesting data. Most important, the questionnaire focused on areas of concern to the industrial buyer. Yet, it would appear that the merchandise buyers who responded to the survey did not have a problem with identifying these concerns. This, in itself, may speak to the similarities between the two sectors' buying processes.

There is little existing research about the behavior of retail buyers. David Mazursky and Elizabeth Hirschman decry this scant attention, because the retail buyer can have such a dramatic effect on the profitability of the firm.[213] Sanford Zimmerman, a former chairman at Abraham & Strauss, is quoted in the *NRMA Buyer's Manual*: "The buyer is the critical factor in the success or failure of any retail venture."[214] Given this importance, it is surprising that such a paucity in the literature exists. This report may help fill that void.

Sample—The sample for the survey reviewed here was drawn from buying personnel at 60 department stores located across the United States. More than 300 questionnaires containing items pertaining to purchasing techniques, buyer training, and buyer performance evaluation were mailed out, and 36 completed responses were returned. While this sample is small, it does represent a diverse group of buying personnel who are geographically dispersed, who are employees of either independently-owned department stores or department store chains, and who fill all levels of the buying hierarchy in department stores. Chains included in the sample were The May Company, Federated Department Stores, Allied, Macy's, Gimbels, Emporium Caldwell, and Associated Dry Goods. Levels represented in the sample ranged from buyers to senior vice presidents responsible for merchandising. Product lines bought by the respondents in this study included home furnishings, cosmetics, lingerie, men's furnishings, ladies' accessories, fashions, men's sportswear, toys, and candy. In addition, respondents' buying experience ranged from one to 36 years with an average of slightly more than 12 years. All in all, the sample obtained from the survey appears to be representative of department store buying personnel.

Results—While this was only an exploratory study aimed at determining some characteristics of merchandise buyers and the merchandise buying process, the results obtained from the survey are instructive and useful for comparison with traditional purchasing practices. For instance, the survey revealed information about vendor evaluation, price determination, professional affiliation, vendor relations, use of long-term contracts, MRO procedures, buyer training, centralization of the buying function, foreign purchasing, other materials functions, use of the computer, and buyer performance evaluation. Each of these is reviewed briefly:

1. Factors used for vendor evaluation. Respondents were asked to rate the importance of the following factors in selecting vendors: quality, timeliness of delivery, price, service, warranty policy, and a miscellaneous category. These criteria are similar to those used by most purchasing agents and, in light of the previous review of the merchandise buying process, would not seem to be an all-inclusive list. However, most respondents seemed to be able to answer this item without much difficulty. In only six cases was the "other" category used. The most frequently used "other" response was a comment relating to fashion, which ties into the previous discussion about the importance of fashion in merchandise buying. In addition, it appears that a number of respondents felt that fashion was part of the quality factor, which was chosen as most important most frequently.

On a scale of one (least important) to five (most important), quality had a mean rating of 4.11 among this sample of department store buyers. Timeliness of delivery followed quality with a mean rating of 3.89. Service had a mean rating of 3.69, followed by price with a mean rating of 3.56. Warranty policy received the lowest mean rating with a score of 2.71. Again, had this item been worded to reflect the importance of returns and markdowns, it probably would have received a higher rating.

Obviously, quality is extremely important to this sample of buyers. However, these results also suggest that delivery, price, and service are also important and, when quality is standardized, become controlling factors in the selection decision. This conclusion is based on the observation that each of these three items had more total ratings of 3.00 and above (moderate and above moderate) than did quality.

These results also dovetail with what is happening in the industrial sector. Greater emphasis is being placed on quality in the source selection decision, but not to the exclusion of price, delivery, and service. As in the industrial sector, some retailers are consolidating their vendor base to ensure more consistent quality in the merchandise they buy. Sear's executives are quoted in *Stores* magazine as intending to "commit their buying strength to fewer and fewer sources, with the emphasis on those that share our concern for intrinsic quality and will work with us on the development of rigid product specifications."[215] The same philosophy is being pursued by those industrial firms who find themselves in a just-in-time environment.

2. Price and vendor selection. This sample of retail buyers more often than not chose vendors on the basis of brand name (64%) and only infrequently used competitive bidding in selecting resources (11%). Another important price factor used in selecting vendors was negotiated discounts (36%). Again, the merchandise buyer is not only a buyer but also a seller of merchandise. How well an item will sell is of paramount importance. Brand names sell and, in many cases, prices on such items are not negotiable. So, while buying on the basis of brand names is frowned upon in the industrial buying office, it would appear to be standard practice among retail buyers. It is interesting to note, however, that among many of the larger department stores, buyers are insisting that manufacturers create exclusive private labels for them, ensuring a competitive edge against the increasing number of specialty stores appearing in the retailing industry. This occurrence may result in the adoption of the Sear's strategy referred to previously. It consists of selecting a few vendors who are willing to work with rigid specifications and exclusive arrangements to ensure competitiveness. Again, this strategy is similar to the one being pursued in the industrial sector, in which many firms purposely reduce their vendor base to ensure better control over quality and delivery.

3. Professional affiliation. One of the more interesting results obtained from this survey of department store buying personnel was that there were no true professional buying associations to which these buyers could belong. When buyers were asked, "Do you or any member of your staff belong to a professional buying association?" they answered by citing the buying group or chain to which they belonged. It is interesting that not one respondent answered the question with "NRMA" (National Retail Merchants Association), a group that more clearly fits the description of a professional association and to which most department stores belong. What is apparent from the responses to this question is that no group fulfills the role of a professional purchasing association for merchandise buyers.

4. Vendor relations. Part of the questionnaire dealt with the issue of ethics. The responses on this part of the survey seemed to indicate that merchandise buyers share the same concerns regarding relationships with vendors as do their industrial counterparts. Diamond and Pintel emphasize that there is an increasing concern with the ethical practices of retail buyers.[216] The recent 1988 report by CAPS on ethical practices demonstrates that this is a common concern shared by all buying professionals.[217] The *NRMA Buyer's Manual* puts this concern in light of the effect that ethical practices can have on the ability of a store to compete: "The practice of ethical business principles and courteous dealings with vendor representatives can mean having the edge in a highly competitive business."[218]

All respondents indicated that their stores had policies relating to professional ethics. Social interaction between buyer and vendor was limited to lunches and dinners, a practice acceptable to 33 percent of the sample. The respondents also felt that accepting token gifts, such as pens and pencils, was acceptable as indicated by their 64-percent favorable response to the question. They drew the line at some gifts; not one of the respondents felt it was ethical to accept the gift of a weekend retreat from a vendor. In short, merchandise buyers appear to have the same ethical standards as those of industrial buyers.

This sample of merchandise buyers mirrors what is reported in the *NRMA Buyer's Manual*, which states that most stores have a policy on gifts. It cautions that the acceptance of gifts could be at worst illegal, since acceptance could be construed as commercial bribery. At best, it is unethical. The manual concludes that the best gift a vendor can give a buyer is well-made, salable merchandise.[219] This sample also mirrors the responses contained in the CAPS study of a wider purchasing population.

The *NRMA Buyer's Manual* delineates what constitutes good and bad ethical practices:

General good business practices:
• Written confirmation of orders
• Good faith in business dealings

Practices to be avoided:
• Undue pressure for cooperative advertising
• Taking of unauthorized or unearned discounts
• Cancellation of definite orders before delivery date
• Unjustified returns
• Pirating of merchandise designs or dealing in pirated designs
• Buying of designer/trademarked merchandise that is actually an illegally copied design.[220]

As noted several times in the previous discussion of retail buying, the success of a retail buyer depends in large measure on the relationships he or she develops with key vendors. Ethical treatment of those resources is clearly one of the ways to ensure good relationships. As noted in the *NRMA Buyer's Manual*, "Good manners and fair courteous treatment should prevail irrespective of how large the order."[221] This advice should be well-heeded regardless of the sector the buyer is operating in.

5. Use of long-term contracts. As would be expected, because of the volatile nature of fashion items, long-term contracts were not used for such items. However, the survey results did indicate that 50 percent of this sample did use contracts of a year or more for the following commodities: men's ready-to-wear, major appliances, MRO items, and cosmetics. As noted earlier, there may be an increasing trend in the use of long-term contracts as retailers attempt to gain greater leverage over their vendor bases and establish exclusive merchandise contracts.

6. MRO purchasing procedures. The responses to the question of how MRO purchases were handled by the store indicate a general lack of awareness by merchandise buyers of such items. The reason is that, in most stores, these items are under the control of the store's purchasing department or maintenance department. There is a distinct dichotomy between merchandising and operations in a department store, and this lack of awareness is not surprising. Most department store purchasing departments have established blanket orders or system contracts for maintenance items and other repetitive supplies purchases. More details concerning the operation of a department store purchasing department are reported in NAPM's 1987 *Guide to Purchasing*.[222]

7. Buyer training. Questions relating to training for both new and experienced buyers illustrate a dichotomy in training programs for buyers in department stores. While respondents indicated that training was considered to be extremely important for new buyers, it appeared that there was little or no formal training for more experienced buyers. This void in training has been noted elsewhere. For instance, R. A. Forrester states that "the retail trade at large still has not recognized the vital importance of training buyers to buy."[223] He further states that this is particularly true in the area of negotiation and points out the value of such training to the profitability of the store.[224]

8. Centralized buying. Like their industrial counterparts, merchandise buyers make use

56

of centralized buying agreements when it is beneficial to their store. In the case of a multibranch store, almost all the respondents (75%) centralized the buying function in the downtown or headquarters store. In addition, 67 percent of this sample of buyers said that they used corporate buying agreements of some form or another when these agreements offered value to the store. Many of the arrangements were in coordination with the import buying office of the parent company or buying group. This situation closely parallels the situation that is found in many multidivision or multiplant industrial firms.

9. Foreign buying. Department stores are extensively engaged in foreign buying. Seventy-nine percent of the respondents in this sample bought offshore. The factors that influenced these buyers to look overseas for merchandise are essentially the same for any buyer. Respondents in this survey indicated that the most important reason for turning to offshore suppliers was quality; 14 of the 36 respondents ranked this factor as most important. Quality was followed by availability and price, which were ranked by 12 respondents each as most important.

The results from this study are very similar to those reported by Diamond and Pintel, who list the following reasons why merchandise buyers turn to offshore resources:

- Lower costs
- Quality
- Greater profit opportunities
- Prestige
- Unavailability of merchandise domestically
- Searching for fashion trends such as haute couture and avant garde fashions.[225]

These factors are very similar to those found by Robert M. Monczka and Larry C. Giunipero in their study of international purchasing by industrial firms.[226] In the retail and industrial sectors, buyers turn offshore because they can find better quality (or perhaps style in the case of merchandise buyers) at more reasonable prices, which in turn allows the buyers' firms to be more competitive in their markets at home.

The leading problem experienced by these buyers when buying offshore was the increased lead times involved with foreign purchases. This was followed by problems with communications, varying quality standards, and currency fluctuations.

Again, Diamond and Pintel cite similar problems:

- Delivery—increased lead times and possible dock strikes
- Quality variations
- Reorders are hard to fill because of lead times
- Necessity for early selection of colors—usually don't get "hot" colors in time to purchase foreign goods
- Size discrepancies
- Money allocation—requires partial payment when order is placed, which ties up capital
- Time involved in foreign buying
- Capital risks as a result of currency exchange rate fluctuation
- Determining the actual cost—need to determine the landed cost of foreign merchandise
- Cost of promotion—foreign goods often unfamiliar to customers and foreign suppliers rarely give promotional allowances.[227]

Again, these problems are similar to the ones encountered by the participants in the Monczka and Giunipero study, which emphasizes the similarities between the two buying processes.

10. Other materials functions. As discussed previously, the texts in retailing generally separate many activities in the procurement process from the buying process itself.[228] It would appear that the sample of merchandise buyers agrees with this assessment because they believed others in the store were responsible for activities such as transportation, expediting, and receiving. In particular, the traffic department was responsible for these activities in most of the stores represented in the sample. Additionally, in most department stores the traffic manager reports to the vice president of operations, a nonmerchandising function.

11. Use of the computer. The computer is used extensively in the retailing business. In the merchandise buying function, it is used for inventory control, maintaining vendor lists, vendor evaluations, and purchase order status. The most heavily used function for the computer is in the area of inventory control. Of the 36 respondents in this sample, 34 indicated that their store used computers for this function. Knowing what is in stock is critical for a merchandise buyer who needs to ensure availability of merchandise in order to ensure sales. Nothing turns off customers more than not being able to find the merchandise that they seek. The inventory control systems in use in many department stores are highly sophisticated, and it is possible that industrial buyers could learn a great deal from their retail counterparts in this area.

12. Buyer evaluation. Performance evaluation is an important topic for merchandise buyers as well as for industrial buyers. In the past, merchandise buyers have been evaluated on the basis of their gross margin. Although gross margin is still an important measure of buyer performance—all 36 respondents in this report indicated that their stores used gross margin in evaluating buyer performance—other measures are now becoming as important. Specifically, other activities that affect total store performance are also being taken into account in measuring buyer performance. In this sample of department store buyers, respondents indicated that such measures as inventory turnover, cost-versus-sales ratios, and operating costs were also being considered. These latter measures are analogous to effectiveness measures now being used to measure industrial buyer behavior. The move away from evaluating retail buyer performance solely on the basis of gross margin parallels the move away from using savings as the primary indicator of industrial buyer performance.

Other studies in the retailing literature have looked at what determines whether a retail buyer will be successful. One such study by Claude R. Martin, Jr., concluded that successful buyers were more aggressive, more self-confident, and more willing to take a leadership role in merchandise trends.[229]

Diamond and Pintel identify the following traits as qualifications for successful merchandise buyers:

- Education
- Enthusiasm
- Analytical excellence
- Ability to articulate
- Product knowledge
- Objective reasoning
- Dedication
- Leadership—not only with people but in fashion
- Appearance
- Flexibility.[230]

These traits are similar to those that are required by industrial purchasing professionals who take a proactive role in the procurement process in their firms.

Retailing Sector Summary

Elizabeth C. Hirschman and David Mazursky suggest that the goals fundamental to the success of a retailer are customer satisfaction and profitability.[231] Clearly, these requirements for success are similar for any firm whether it be in the retail or industrial sector. Critical to the success of any retailer are the actions of its merchandise buyers because, as noted in the NRMA Buyer's Manual, "successful retailing depends on locating profitable sources of supply and maintaining dealings with them as long as a profit is shown."[232]

As the dollars spent by industrial firms on the purchase of goods and services increases (some firms are already spending 65 percent of their total sales dollars on these items), the role of their suppliers in their success can only increase. This trend also means that the role of the industrial buyer in a firm's success is also increasing. And, as noted by Dobler, Lee, and Burt, buyer success is clearly a function of the success of the firm's suppliers.[233]

As noted in this review of the merchandise buying process, many of the methods used to ensure success are similar in both sectors. Diamond and Pintel clearly describe what it takes for a merchandise buyer to be successful. They emphasize that strong supplier relationships can be achieved by placing significant volumes with a few suppliers and by treating these suppliers, as well as all suppliers, fairly and ethically.[234] Again, fair and ethical treatment of suppliers by buyers applies across all sectors.

So, while there may be some critical differences between industrial buying and retail buying, similarities do appear. The common thread that runs through the buying processes in all sectors is that good buying is good buying.

SUMMARY: GOOD BUYING IS GOOD BUYING

What this extensive review of the buying processes in the various sectors of the economy indicates is that the goals of buyers in all sectors are essentially identical; that is, all buyers are interested in buying goods and services that meet the needs of their customers at the lowest possible total cost. The methods used by each sector to obtain this goal may differ somewhat, but the methods are similar to each other, too. The major concerns of buyers in all sectors are quite similar and are discussed below.

Goals and Processes

The goals of all buyers are essentially the same. Goods are bought to satisfy the needs of customers. This includes internal customers of the industrial, institutional, and governmental buyer, and the company's customers in the case of retail buyers. While this may seem to be a major difference between the purchase of goods for resale and those that are not for resale, it is interesting that many industrial buyers are becoming more cognizant of their final customer's needs as well. Consider, for example, that a number of newer evaluations of quality in the industrial firm take account of customer satisfaction. In buying for resale or not for resale, quality is becoming more and more important. And, in both cases, quality can be measured in terms of how well the purchase satisfies the customer's needs. So, a goal of both the retail buyer and the industrial buyer is customer satisfaction.

The processes followed by each sector also demonstrate similarities. In all cases, a need is identified, qualified sources are located and asked to make proposals, the best source is chosen and terms and conditions of a contract are negotiated, and performance of the chosen supplier is monitored for conformance to the contract. In all sectors, supplier evaluations have been developed to aid in this process.

No matter how specific goals may be expressed and processes carried out, it is clear from this review that good buying is good buying. Or, as the old adage states, "goods well bought are half sold." This applies to purchasing in any sector.

Structure

Another similarity shown in this review of purchasing across sectors is the commonality in organizational form used to organize buying activities. In almost all cases, a combination of centralization and decentralization is used to organize these activities. The value of centralizing certain purchases has been demonstrated as a principle of good buying regardless of sector. At the same time, flexibility dictates the need for some level of decentralization in which economies of scale are not obtained through corporate contracts.

Reliable Suppliers

The key to good buying in all sectors discussed in this review is the ability to select, develop, and maintain reliable suppliers. With this in mind, all sectors, except the governmental sector, have sought to develop better relationships with their supplier bases by looking upon them as extensions of their own companies. Even in the government sector, buyers have realized that greater cooperation with suppliers will result in better purchasing.

One of the methods that has been used by most companies in developing better relationships with their supplier bases is to reduce the number of suppliers they do business with and to enter into longer-term agreements with these suppliers. In many cases, companies are electing to engage in single-source relationships and are looking at their suppliers as partners who are willing to go the extra mile in terms of service, design, quality, and price.

A Professional Work Force

Another key to good buying is the development of a highly qualified and professional work force. In order to achieve such a lofty goal, buyers in all sectors have turned to professional organizations for ways to improve themselves. With the exception of the retail sector, each of the other sectors has an organization (or organizations) that fills these needs:

SECTOR	PROFESSIONAL ORGANIZATION
Industrial	National Association of Purchasing Management (NAPM)
	American Production and Inventory Control Society (APICS)
Institutional	National Association of Educational Buyers (NAEB)
	American Society for Hospital Materials Management (ASHMM)
Governmental	
Federal	National Contract Management Association (NCMA)
State and	National Institute of Governmental Purchasing (NIGP)
Local	National Association of State Purchasing Officials (NASPO)

While retail buyers do not have a separate professional organization, most are actively involved with the National Retail Merchants Association (NRMA), which provides training for buyers along with a myriad of other programs offered to improve all areas of retail organizations.

A more detailed listing of professional purchasing associations is listed in Exhibit 3.

In an attempt to improve the professionalism of their members, each of these organizations has developed educational and training programs that lead to professional certification. As noted in Table 1 in the beginning of this report, about one-third of the members of these organizations have obtained certifications. Each association is also actively lobbying organizations who employ their members to insist on certification as a condition of employment and/or promotion in the purchasing field. It is believed that certification programs will lead to a more highly trained work force sought by both profit and not-for-profit organizations.

The statistics in Table 1 also show an increasing level of education being achieved by buyers in all sectors. The increase has occurred partly because many organizations require college degrees for entry-level purchasing positions.

EXHIBIT 3
PROFESSIONAL PURCHASING ASSOCIATIONS

Name of Organization	Members	Staff	Annual Budget	Annual Membership Fee	Type Ind.	Type Org.	Certification
American Society for Hospital Materials Management	2,000	3	$100,000-$250,000	$75	X		
National Association of Educational Buyers	2,200	6	$500,000-$1 million			X	C.P.M.(Certified Purchasing Manager)
National Association of Purchasing Management	31,000	29	$2 million-$5 million	$60	X		C.P.M. (Certified Purchasing Manager)
National Association of State Purchasing Officials	100-125	2	$100,000-$250,000	$800	X		
National Contract Management Association	23,000	30	$2 million-$5 million	$60	X		C.A.C.M. (CertifiedAssociate Contract Manager) C.P.C.M. (Certified Purchasing Contract Manager)
National Institute of Governmental Purchasing	1,500	10-13	$500,000-$1 million	$150-$300		X	C.P.P.O. (Certified Public Purchasing Officer)
National Retail Merchants Association	45,000	90-100	$5 million+			X	
American Production and Inventory Control Society	(Individuals) 66,000 (Companies) 1,100	67	$5 million+	$85	X		C.P.I.M. (Certified in Production and Inventory Management)

Source: *National Trade and Professional Associations of the United States* (22nd edition), Washington, D.C.: Columbia Books, Inc., 1990.

Exhibit 3 gives additional information about the professional purchasing associations across the various sectors.

Improved Purchasing Methods

This review of purchasing across sectors has also demonstrated the pursuit of better purchasing through improved buying practices:

- For instance, this review has shown that all sectors use some form of value analysis to ensure that appropriate products are being specified.
- All sectors use specification buying to some degree to ensure clear communication to suppliers and conformance to quality expectations.
- Make-or-buy decisions are conducted in each sector to ensure the most effective utilization of resources.
- And, whenever possible, buying organizations attempt to purchase standardized items to ensure economical purchases.

Additionally, buyers in all sectors have turned to improved purchasing procedures to obtain the maximum efficiency from their buying activities. These efficiency measures include such things as the use of single-order sourcing from master distributors for a myriad of high-volume, low-value items. Such actions result in decreased inventory, orders, and deliveries of such items resulting in decreased acquisition costs. Other examples of such methods include systems contracting, and check-with-order. The methods are aimed at reducing the time that buyers spend handling activities associated with routine, repetitive purchases.

The use of new information technology is also a common thread to good buying in all sectors. Such things as EDI, buyer workstations, the use of FAX, and other examples of computerization have facilitated greater purchasing effectiveness by buyers.

Cost Containment

In their efforts to hold the line on costs, most organizations have come to realize the importance of their purchasing departments in attaining this goal. Good buying results in lower costs. The key to achieving this goal is the early involvement of purchasing in the procurement process so as to ensure

that good buying occurs. This is perhaps the most important common goal of buyers in all sectors. Except for the retailing sector, many buyers are still struggling to achieve this goal of early involvement.

Good Buying: The Differences

Obviously, the buying process differs in each sector. The differences include the closeness of the retail buyer to his or her final customer. The procedural detail involved in government procurement is also a major difference.

In the case of the retail buyer's relationship to his or her final customer, it may be that this difference is not so great as it once was. As noted earlier, industrial buyers are becoming involved with final customers before buying component parts and raw materials in order to ensure conformance to customer needs. In any sector, final customer satisfaction is the key to success, and the only way to ensure such success is to know the customer better.

In addition, many industrial purchasers are involved in selling. This is a result of the increasing use of countertrades in the selling of products to developing countries. In fact, some industrial firms have included export trading as part of a supply department that also includes the purchasing function. Another example of buyers who have responsibility for selling is found in the institutional purchasing departments at many universities. In many cases, these departments have responsibility for the campus bookstore.

Government procurement is usually characterized by procedural detail. In reality, procedural detail exists in the private sector, too. Given the amount of business the government does at all levels, what affects purchasing in the public sector spills over to the private sector. In order to comply with government legislation that relates to selling to the government, federal contractors must ensure that their buying departments are in full compliance with these laws. In short, government procurement legislation has the effect of controlling most buying regardless of the sector. Additionally, the government, and professional associations associated with government procurement, are attempting to have their buyers act like their industrial counterparts in letting the marketplace, rather than procedural detail, dictate buying decisions. However, they still have a long way to go.

Each sector has unique purchases that require special handling. But even here, such uniqueness could be found between different industrial firms. These differences result more from a firm's purpose rather than the sector it belongs to.

Finally, one major difference that does occur between profit and not-for-profit purchasing is the use of buying cooperatives. Clearly, one of the essentials of good buying is the attainment of buying leverage. Since many not-for-profit organizations are unable to obtain buying leverage on their own, they bind together and group their purchases to obtain better prices. Because of their not-for-profit status, legal authorities have seemed to allow these combinations, but the combinations are now becoming more susceptible to challenge by sellers who feel they are at a disadvantage under such arrangements. Since the purchases made by the not-for-profit sector are growing so rapidly, it may well be that some of these challenges may begin to find a sympathetic ear in the legal system.

In any case, one sector's procurement function differs only slightly from another's—there are not significant difference across sectors. This means that a common body of purchasing knowledge is applicable to all sectors with some modification required for each particular situation. This also suggests that there really could be a single professional body of buyers all in pursuit of a single goal—good buying.

REFERENCES

[1]See for example, Donald W. Dobler, Lamar Lee, Jr., and David N. Burt, *Purchasing and Materials Management* (New York: McGraw-Hill), Fourth edition, 1984, p. 4.

[2]Ibid.
In June 1990, full-time Contractors, Purchasing Agents, and Purchasing Clerical Assistants (job codes 1102, 1105, and 1106, respectively) in the Department of Defense totaled 35,111. Figure provided by Defense Manpower Data Center, Monterey, California.

[3]U.S. Department of Labor, Bureau of Labor Statistics, *Occupational Outlook Handbook 1986-87 Edition,* Bulletin 2250, April 1986.

[4]"Projections 2000: Occupational Employment," *Monthly Labor Review,* September 1987, p. 51.

[5]Personal Communication with Mr. Wayne Wittig, Department of Defense, and Professor Harry Page, The George Washington University.

[6]David Chance, *Profile of the N.A.P.M. Membership* (Oradell, New Jersey: The National Association of Purchasing Management) January 1986.

[7]Curtis R. Cook, *A Study of Decision-Making Processes in the Practice of Federal Contract Management* (unpublished doctoral dissertation, The George Washington University) July 1987.

[8]Larry C. Giunipero and Lee Stepina, Executive Summary: Hospital Materials Management Survey (unpublished manuscript, Florida State University) September 1985.

[9]Michael G. Kolchin and Larry C. Giunipero, "Merchandise and Industrial Buying: A Comparison," in *Current Research in Purchasing and Materials Management*, eds. Joseph R. Carter and Gary L. Ragatz (East Lansing, Michigan: Michigan State University), October 1987, pp. 184-194.

[10]David Chance, *Profile of the NAPM Membership* (Tempe, Arizona: The National Association of Purchasing Management) January 1989.

[11]I.V. Fine and J.H. Westing, "Organizational Characteristics of Purchasing Personnel in Public and Private Hierarchies," *Journal of Purchasing,* August 1973, pp. 5-12.

[12]Ibid., p. 11.

[13]Chance, 1986, op. cit., p. 1.

[14]Chance, 1989, op. cit., p. 1.
Compare the 25 percent female membership of NAPM (1989) with the 65.8 percent females among full-time Department of Defense (1990) Contractors, Purchasing Agents, and Purchasing Clerical Assistants (job codes 1102, 1105, and 1106, respectively). Figure provided by the Defense Manpower Data Center, Monterey, California.

[15]Ibid.

[16]See J.M. Rehfisch, "A Scale for Personal Rigidity," *Journal of Consulting Psychology,* Vol. 22, 1958, pp. 10-15, R.J. House and J.R. Rizzo, "Toward the Measurement of Organizational Practices," *Journal of Applied Psychology,* Vol. 56, 1972, pp. 388-396, and R.J. House and G. Dessler, "The Path-Goal Theory of Leadership: Some Post Hoc and A Priori Tests," in J.G. Hunt and J.M. Sprague (eds.) *Contingency Approaches to Leadership* (Carbondale, Illinois: Southern Illinois University Press) 1974, pp. 29-55.

[17]"Purchasing," *Hospitals,* January 20, 1987, p. 100.

[18]David S. Greisler and Sumer C. Aggarwal, "Hospital Materials Management: Potential for Improvement," *Journal of Purchasing and Materials Management,* Spring 1985, p. 18.

[19]Dean S. Ammer, *Purchasing and Materials Management for Health-Care Institutions* (Lexington, Massachusetts: Lexington Books) 1975, p. 2.

[20]Dean S. Ammer, *Purchasing and Materials Management for Health-Care Institutions,* Second edition (Lexington, Massachusetts: Lexington Books) 1983.

[21]Greisler and Aggarwal, op. cit., p. 17.

[22]J.P. Widman, "Development of a Prudent Purchasing Program," in Charles E. Housley (ed.), *Hospital Purchasing: Focus on Effectiveness* (Rockville, Maryland: Aspen Publications) 1983, p. 96.

[23]M.H. Goodloe, "The Effects of the Prudent Buyer Concept on the Supplier," in Charles E. Housley (ed.), *Hospital Purchasing: Focus on Effectiveness* (Rockville, Maryland: Aspen Publications) 1983, p. 110.

[24]W.K. Henning, "Application of the Prudent Buyer Principle to Purchasing Administration," in Charles E. Housley (ed.), *Hospital Purchasing: Focus on Effectiveness* (Rockville, Maryland: Aspen Publications) 1983, p. 100.

[25] Greisler and Aggarwal, op. cit., p. 20.

[26] J.H. Holmgren and W.J. Wentz, *Material Management and Purchasing for the Health Care Facility* (Ann Arbor, Michigan: AUPHA Press) 1982, pp. 6-7.

[27] J.J. Frommelt and J.L. Schanilec, "The Integration of Central Services into Material Management," in J.H. Holmgren and W.J. Wentz, *Material Management and Purchasing for the Health Care Facility* (Ann Arbor, Michigan: AUPHA Press) 1982, p. 167.

[28] Holmgren and Wentz, op. cit., p. 4.

[29] Giunipero and Stepina, op. cit., p. 12.

[30] Holmgren and Wentz, op. cit., p. 5.

[31] S. Randolph Hayas, "Total Centralized Purchasing: Can It Ever Be Achieved," in Charles E. Housley (ed.), *Hospital Purchasing: Focus on Effectiveness* (Rockville, Maryland: Aspen Publications) 1983, p. 31.

[32] Holmgren and Wentz, op. cit., p. 276.

[33] C.E. Housley, "Overcoming Barriers to Group Purchasing," in Charles E. Housley (ed.), *Hospital Purchasing: Focus on Effectiveness* (Rockville, Maryland: Aspen Publications) 1983, p. 227.

[34] C.W. Moore, "Group Purchasing: Past, Present and Future," in Charles E. Housley (ed.), *Hospital Purchasing: Focus on Effectiveness* (Rockville, Maryland: Aspen Publications) 1983, p. 243.

[35] C.E. Housley, "The Prime Supplier Contract: Getting the Most For the Hospital's Supply Dollar," in Charles E. Housley (ed.), *Hospital Purchasing: Focus on Effectiveness* (Rockville, Maryland: Aspen Publications) 1983, p. 125.

[36] Holmgren and Wentz, op. cit., p. 73.

[37] Holmgren and Wentz, op. cit., p. 25.

[38] Goodloe, op. cit., p. 114.

[39] R. Dan Reid and Carl D. Riegel, *Purchasing Practices of Large Foodservice Firms* (Tempe, Arizona: Center for Advanced Purchasing Studies/ National Association of Purchasing Management, Inc.) 1989, pp. 76.

[40] Reid and Riegel, op. cit., p. 20.

[41] Dobler, Lee, and Burt, op. cit., p. 55.

[42] Reid and Riegel, op. cit., p. 18.

[43] Harold E. Fearon, *Purchasing Organizational Relationships* (Tempe, Arizona: Center for Advanced Purchasing Studies/National Association of Purchasing Management, Inc.) 1988, p. 16.

[44] Hugh J. Kelly, *Food Service Purchasing: Principles and Practices* (New York: Chain Store Publishing Corporation) 1976, p. 184.

[45] Reid and Riegel, op. cit., p. 23.

[46] Ibid., p. 26.

[47] Robert L. Janson, *Purchasing Ethical Practices* (Tempe, Arizona: Ernst and Whinney/Center for Advanced Purchasing Studies/National Association of Purchasing Management, Inc.) 1988, p. 10.

[48] Reid and Riegel, op. cit., p. 17, and Fearon, op. cit., pp. 17-20.

[49] Reid and Riegel, op. cit., p. 21.

[50] Clark L. Bernard and Douglas Beaven, "Containing the Costs of Higher Education," *Journal of Accounting,* Vol. 160, No. 4 (October), 1985, pp. 78-92.

[51] Ibid., p. 78.

[52] Ibid., p. 80.

[53] Ibid., p. 84.

[54] Ibid.

[55] James J. Ritterskamp, Jr., Forrest L. Abbott, and Bert C. Ahrens, *Purchasing for Educational Institutions* (New York: Bureau of Publications, Teacher's College, Columbia University) 1961, p. 39.

[56] Bernard and Beaven, op. cit., p. 84.

[57] Ibid., p. 90.

[58] Ibid., p. 86.

[59] Ritterskamp et al., op. cit., p. 203.

[60] U.S. Bureau of the Census, *Statistical Abstract of the United States:* 1988, p. 119.

[61] Ibid., p. 88.

[62] Donald W. Dobler, David N. Burt, and Lamar Lee, Jr., *Purchasing and Materials Management* (New York: McGraw-Hill) Fifth edition, 1990, p. 660.

[63] Unpublished survey conducted by Gerald F. Evans, Director of Purchasing and Stores, University of Arizona, Tucson, Arizona, 1987.

[64] Dobler, Burt, and Lee, op. cit., p. 616.

[65] Ritterskamp et al., op. cit., p. 22.

[66] Herman Holtz, "The $650 Billion Market Opportunity," *Business Marketing,* Vol. 71, No. 10, (October) 1986, p. 88.

[67]Harry Robert Page, *Public Purchasing and Materials Management* (Lexington, Massachusetts: Lexington Books) 1980, p. xiii.

[68]*State and Local Government Purchasing* (Lexington, Kentucky: The Council of State Governments), 1975, p. 1.1.

[69]Stanley N. Sherman, *Government Procurement Management* (Gaithersburg, Maryland: Wordcrafters Publications), Second edition, 1985, p. iii.

[70]Dobler, Burt, and Lee, op. cit., p. 678-679.

[71]"The Defense Scandal," *Business Week*, July 4, 1988, pp. 28-33.

[72]*The Federal Procurement Process* (Washington, D.C.: U.S. Office of Management and Budget, Office of Procurement Policy, Task Group Number 3, The Executive Committee on Federal Procurement Reform) November 16, 1983.

[73]Page, op. cit., p. 262.

[74]Ibid., p. 9.

[75]Sherman, op. cit., pp. 222.

[76]Curtis R. Cook, *A Study of Decision-Making Processes in the Practice of Federal Contract Management* (unpublished doctoral dissertation, The George Washington University) July 1987, p. 11.

[77]U.S. Office of Management and Budget, Office of Federal Procurement Policy, *Proposal for a Uniform Federal Procurement System* (Washington, D.C.: Government Printing Office) 1982, p. v.

[78]Bruce van Voorst, "Mission: Just About Impossible," *Time,* February 1, 1988, p. 44.

[79]Sherman, op. cit., p. 27.

[80]Summary of DOD Procurement Process prepared for Dr. Robert B. Costello, Assistant Secretary of Defense for Acquisitions and Logistics, by the Office of the Assistant Secretary of Defense, Acquisition and Logistics (Policy), 1987.

[81]Sherman, op. cit., p. 20.

[82]Ibid., p. 334.

[83]Ronald L. Schill, "Buying Practices in the U.S. Department of Defense," *Industrial Marketing,* Vol. 9, 1980, p. 291.

[8]Jagdish N. Sheth, Robert F. Williams, and Richard M. Hill, "Government and Business Purchasing: How Similar Are They?" *Journal of Purchasing and Material Management,* Vol. 19, No. 4, Winter 1983, p. 8.

[85]Dobler, Lee, and Burt, op. cit., p. 647.

[86]Sherman, op. cit., p. 52.

[87]Dobler, Lee, and Burt, op. cit., p. 669.

[88]Sheth et al., op. cit., p. 12.

[89]Ibid., pp. 9-12.

[90]Sherman, op. cit., p. 121.

[91]Ibid., pp. 367-375.

[92]*Proposal for a Uniform Federal Procurement System,* op. cit., p. 13.

[93]Sherman, op. cit., p. 240.

[94]Dobler, Burt, and Lee, op. cit., pp. 204-205.

[95]Sherman, op. cit., p. 52.

[96]Ibid., p. 235.

[97]Ibid., p. 376.

[98]Sheth et al., op. cit., pp. 12-13.

[99]Ibid., p. 7.

[100]Schill, op. cit., p. 294.

[101]Sherman, op. cit., pp. 139-140.

[102]Ibid., p. 154.

[103]Ibid., p. 159.

[104]Ibid., p. 357.

[105]*Proposal for a Uniform Federal Procurement System,* op. cit., p. 133.

[106]Report of the Secretary of Defense Caspar W. Weinberger to the Congress on the FY 1988/FY 1989 Budget and FY 1988-92 Defense Programs, January 12, 1987, p. 103.

[107]Sherman, op. cit., p. 100.

[108]*Proposal for a Uniform Federal Procurement System,* op. cit., p. v.

[109]Ibid., p. 6.

[110]Ibid., p. 110.

[111]Page, op. cit., p. 35.

[112]Sherman, op. cit., p. 121.

[113]Colleen A. Preston, "Congress and the Acquisition Process: Some Recommendations for Improvement," *NCMA Journal,* Vol. 20, No. 1, Summer 1986, p. 24.

[114]Sherman, op. cit., p. 134.

[115]Robert F. Williams and V. Sagar Bakhshi, "Competitive Bidding: Department of Defense and Private Sector Practices," *Journal of Purchasing and Materials Management,* Vol. 24, No. 3, Fall 1988, p. 34.

[116]Ibid., p. 33.

[117]Ibid., p. 34.

[118]James E. Colvard and Alan W. Beck, "Cost of Object or Object of Cost?" *The Bureaucrat,* Vol. 14, No. 2, Winter 1985-86, p. 19.

[119]Ibid., p. 22.

[120]Michael N. Beltramo and Anthony J. Deluca, "Is Competition Hurting Technology?" *Military Logistics Forum,* Vol. 4, No. 3, pp. 42-49.

[121]Ibid., p. 48.

[122]Ibid., p. 44.

[123]Ibid., p. 49.

[124]"Rear Admiral Stuart F. Platt, the Navy's Costbuster," *S&MM* {Sales & Marketing Management}, March 10, 1986, pp. 45-47.

[125]Van Voorst, op. cit., p. 44.

[126]"Defense Procurement: Killed in Action," *The Economist,* October 17, 1987, p. 33.

[127]Diane Norman, "Godwin Says He Lacked Clear Mandate for Reform," *Electronic Buyers' News,* September 29, 1987, p. 1.

[128]Ibid.

[129]The President's Blue Ribbon Commission on Defense Management," *A Formula for Action: A Report to the President on Defense Acquisition,* Washington, D.C.: Government Printing Office, 1986 and Executive Order 12352 of March 17, 1982, 47 FR 12125, 3 CFR, 1982 Comp., p. 137.

[130]*A Formula for Action: A Report to the President on Defense Acquisition,* op. cit., pp. 12-13.

[131]Ibid., pp. 15-16.

[132]Page, op. cit., p. 7.

[133]Sherman, op. cit., p. 383.

[134]Colvard and Beck, op. cit., p. 22.

[135]National Contract Management Association (NCMA), *Education and Training Program Structure,* January 1985.

[136]Department of Defense, The Acquisition Enhancement (ACEII) Study Group, *The Acquisition Enhancement (ACE) Program Report II,* Volume 1, December 1986.

[137]Federal Acquisition Institute, Office of Acquisition Policy, General Services Administration, *Government Wide Study of Procurement Training,* September 1987.

[138]"Civilian Procurement Corps Proposal Boosts Job Chances," *Impact,* Vol. 1, No. 1, September 1989, p. 1.

[139]United States General Accounting Office, Report to Congressional Requesters, *Procurement Personnel: Information on the Procurement Workforce,* November 1987, p. 19.

[140]"C.P.M. Status Gives Purchasers an Edge when Seeking GS-1102 Positions," *Impact,* Vol. 1, No. 4, December 1989, p. 2.

[141]Cook, op. cit., p. 13.

[142]Ibid., p. 153.

[143]Speech presented by the Honorable Robert B. Costello, Assistant Secretary of Defense (Production and Logistics), at the National East Coast Educational Conference of the National Contract Management Association, November 6, 1987, p. 18.

[144]Dick Cheney, Secretary of Defense, "A Plan to Improve the Defense Acquisitions Process and Management of the Pentagon," *Defense 89,* Special issue (Washington, D.C.: GPO, 1989), pp. 8-9.

[145]Department of Defense, *Defense Management Report Implementation Progress Report* (Washington, D.C.: GPO, 1990), p. 2.

[146]*A Guide to the New United States Postal Service Procurement Manual,* United States Postal Service, October 1987, p. 1.

[147]Carla S. Lallatin, "Sales Opportunities in State and Local Government Markets," *Agency Sales Magazine,* Vol. 17, No. 2, February 1987, p. 51.

[148]Page, op. cit., p. 1.

[149]Ibid., pp. 8-9.

[150]*Results of the 1983 Procurement Survey* (Falls Church, Virginia: National Institute of Governmental Purchasing, Inc.) 1983, p. 2.

[151]*Results of the 1989 Procurement Survey* (Falls Church, Virginia: National Institute of Governmental Purchasing, Inc.) 1989, p. 3.

[152]The Council of State Governments, *State and Local Government Purchasing* (Lexington, Kentucky: Council of State Governments/National Association of State Purchasing Officials), Second edition, 1983, pp. 186-187.

[153]*Results of the 1983 Procurement Survey,* op. cit., p. 2.

[154]*Results of the 1989 Procurement Survey,* op. cit., p. 5.

[155] *State and Local Government Purchasing:* A Digest (Lexington, Kentucky: The Council of State Governments) 1974, pp. 4-5.

[156] *State and Local Government Purchasing* (Lexington, Kentucky: The Council of State Governments) 1975, p. 2.1.

[157] *State and Local Government Purchasing,* Second edition, 1983, op. cit., pp. 17 + ___.

[158] *Results of the 1989 Procurement Survey,* op. cit., pp. 4-5.

[159] *Results of the 1983 Procurement Survey,* op. cit., p. 3.

[160] *State and Local Government Purchasing,* Second edition, 1983, op. cit., p. 124.

[161] *Results of the 1983 Procurement Survey,* op. cit., p. 3.

[162] Ibid.

[163] *Results of the 1989 Procurement Survey,* op. cit., p. 18.

[164] *State and Local Government Purchasing,* Second edition, op. cit., p. 140.

[165] *Results of the 1983 Procurement Survey,* op. cit., p. 3.

[166] *State and Local Government Purchasing,* Second edition, op. cit., p. 140.

[167] *Results of the 1989 Procurement Survey,* op. cit., p. 13.

[168] *Results of the 1983 Procurement Survey,* op. cit., p. 4.

[169] *Results of the 1989 Procurement Survey,* op. cit., p. 16.

[170] *State and Local Government Purchasing,* Second edition, op. cit., p. 153.

[171] *Results of the 1983 Procurement Survey,* op. cit., p. 4.

[172] *State and Local Government Purchasing,* Second edition, op. cit., p. 229.

[173] *Results of the 1983 Procurement Survey,* op. cit., p. 3.

[174] *Results of the 1989 Procurement Survey,* op. cit., p. 7.

[175] Page, op. cit., p. 317.

[176] *Results of the 1989 Procurement Survey,* op. cit., p. 12.

[177] Chance, 1989, op. cit., p. 3.

[178] *State and Local Government Purchasing,* Second edition, op. cit., p. 237.

[179] *Results of the 1989 Procurement Survey,* op. cit., p. 12.

[180] *State and Local Government Purchasing,* Second edition, op. cit., pp. 218-220.

[181] Janson, op. cit., pp. 26-27.

[182] *State and Local Government Purchasing,* Second edition, op. cit., p. 213.

[183] *State and Local Government Purchasing:* A Digest, op. cit.

[184] Janice Davis, "B.C. Launches Supplynet System," *Computing Canada,* Vol. 12, No. 18, September 4, 1986, pp. 1-2.

[185] *Results of the 1989 Procurement Survey,* op. cit., p. 19.

[186] *State and Local Government Purchasing,* op. cit., p. ix.

[187] *State and Local Government Purchasing:* A Digest, op. cit., p. 30.

[188] Dobler, Burt, and Lee, op. cit., p. 4.

[189] Richard Ettenson and Janet Wagner, "Retail Buyers' Saleability Judgements: A Comparison of Information Use Across Levels of Experience," *Journal of Retailing,* Vol. 62, No. 1, 1986, p. 42.

[190] Therese M. Maskulka, *An Examination of Strategic Planning in Retailing* (unpublished doctoral dissertation, Kent State University) 1987.

[191] D.M. Lewison and M.W. DeLozier, *Retailing* (Columbus, Ohio: Merrill), Fourth edition, 1986, p. 476.

[192] Gary J. Zenz, *Purchasing and the Management of Materials* (New York: Wiley), Sixth edition, 1987, pp. 7-10.

[193] David N. Burt, *Proactive Procurement* (Englewood Cliffs, New Jersey: Prentice-Hall) 1984, p. 3.

[194] Ibid., p. 23.

[195] Jay Diamond and Gerald Pintel, *Retail Buying* (Englewood Cliffs, New Jersey: Prentice-Hall), Third edition, 1989, pp. 7-9.

[196] Ibid., p. 2.

[197] Ibid., p. 33.

[198] R. Patrick Cash, *The Buyer's Manual* (New York: National Retail Merchants Association) 1979.

[199] Ibid., p. 100.

[200]Michael Levy and Michael VanBreda, "How to Determine Whether to Buy Direct or Through a Wholesaler," *Retail Control,* Vol. 53, No. 9, June-July 1985, p. 42.

[201]Cash, op. cit., p. 64.

[202]Ibid., p. 127.

[203]Ibid., p. 130.

[204]Edwin Crooks, "The Case for Concentrating Purchases," *Journal of Retailing,* Vol. 42, No. 2, 1966, pp. 14-18.

[205]Arch G. Woodside, "Reseller Buying Behavior: Some Questions and Tentative Answers," in J.H. Summey and R.D. Taylor (eds.), *Evolving Marketing Thought for 1980: Proceedings of the Annual Meeting of the Southern Marketing Association* (New Orleans, Louisiana), November 19-22, 1980, p. 495.

[206]Lewison and DeLozier, op. cit., pp. 487-89.

[207]Cash, op. cit., pp. 128-129.

[208]Diamond and Pintel, op. cit., pp. 149-154.

[209]John S. Berens, "A Decision Matrix Approach to Supplier Selection," *Journal of Retailing,* Vol. 47, No. 4, Winter 1971-1972, pp. 47-53.

[210]Diamond and Pintel, op. cit., p. 159.

[211]Cash, op. cit., pp. 131-132.

[212]Ibid., p. 132.

[213]David Mazursky and Elizabeth Hirschman, "A Cross-Organisational Comparison of Retail Buyers: Information Source Utilisation," *International Journal of Retailing,* Vol. 2, No. 1, 1987, p. 44.

[214]Cash, op. cit., p. 42.

[215]"NRMA News," *Stores,* Vol. 62, No. 3, 1980, p. 58.

[216]Diamond and Pintel, op. cit., p. 166.

[217]Janson, op. cit., p. 6.

[218]Cash, op. cit., pp. 132-133.

[219]Ibid.

[220]Ibid., pp. 130-131.

[221]Ibid., pp. 129-130.

[222]Michael G. Kolchin, "Purchasing for the Department Store," in *Guide to Purchasing* (2.15) (Oradell, New Jersey: National Association of Purchasing Management, Inc.), 1987.

[223]R.A. Forrester, "Buying for Profitability," *Retail and Distribution Management,* Vol. 15, No. 3, May/June 1987, p. 25.

[224]Ibid., p. 26.

[225]Diamond and Pintel, op. cit., pp. 200-204.

[226]Robert M. Monczka and Larry C. Giunipero, "International Purchasing: Characteristics and Implementations," *Journal of Purchasing and Materials Management,* Vol. 20, No. 3, Fall 1984, pp. 2-9.

[227]Diamond and Pintel, op. cit., pp. 204-208.

[228]Lewison and DeLozier, op. cit., pp. 474-525.

[229]Claude R. Martin, Jr., "The Contribution of the Professional Buyer to a Store's Success or Failure," *Journal of Retailing,* Vol. 49, No. 2, Summer 1973, p. 79.

[230]Diamond and Pintel, op. cit., pp. 13-16.

[231]Elizabeth C. Hirschman and David Mazursky, "A Trans-Organizational Investigation of Retail Buyers' Criteria and Information Sources," *New York University Institute of Retail Management Working Paper No. 82-8* (New York: New York University Graduate School of Business Administration), 1982, p. 44.

[232]Cash, op. cit., p. 132.

[233]Dobler, Lee, and Burt, op. cit., p. 123.

[234]Diamond and Pintel, op. cit., p. 167.

APPENDIX: COVER LETTER AND SURVEY •

Lehigh University   *Department of Management*
                          and Marketing

College of Business and Economics
Drown Hall 35
Bethlehem, Pennsylvania 18015
telephone (215) 861-3441

Dear Fellow Purchasing Professional:

I am currently conducting a study on the nature of purchasing
positions in both industrial and institutional purchasing. I
would greatly appreciate it if you would take fifteen or twenty
minutes to complete the attached survey and return it to me in the
enclosed, stamped, return envelope.

It is my hope to collect this data in the next several weeks
so I would appreciate it if you would respond as soon as possible.
After I have collected the data and analyzed it, I will be preparing
a report which I intend to present to a professional meeting next
year. If you so desire, I will be happy to provide you with a copy
of this report. At the end of the survey, there is a place for you
to check to indicate that you would like a copy.

Please be sure to respond to all items on the survey. Also,
please be assured that your responses will be treated confidentially.
The published results of this survey will only present composite
pictures of industrial and institutional buyers.

Thank you very much for taking the time to participate in this
study. Your cooperation will allow us to enhance the professionalism
and effectiveness of the purchasing profession.

Sincerely,

Michael G. Kolchin
Assistant Professor of Management
and
Director of Professional Development
Purchasing Management Association
of the Lehigh Valley, Inc.

MGK/jc

Purchasing Survey

General Instructions:

You are being asked to participate in a study concerning the nature of the purchasing function. The questionnaire that follows asks a series of questions relating to yourself, your job as a purchasing professional, your company, and your immediate supervisor. All responses you make on this questionnaire will be treated confidentially and will not be available to others. As you read each item below, please check or circle the first response that comes to mind. Also, please insure that you respond to all items and please be as candid as possible.

Part I: Self Evaluation

Instructions:

This portion of the questionnaire contains a series of statements relating to you personally. Read each one, decide how you feel about it, and then check your answer in the space provided. There are seven (7) possible responses captioned as follows: Strongly Disagree; Disagree; Slightly Disagree; Neither Agree nor Disagree; Slightly Agree; Agree; and Strongly Agree. Check the most appropriate response for each item. Please be sure to answer all statements being as candid as possible.

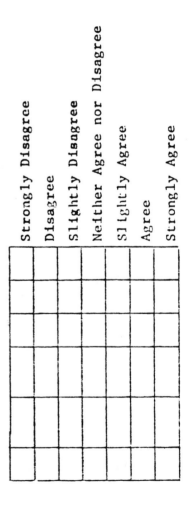

	Strongly Disagree	Disagree	Slightly Disagree	Neither Agree nor Disagree	Slightly Agree	Agree	Strongly Agree
1. I must admit that it makes me angry when other people interfere with my daily activity.							
2. I find that a well-ordered mode of life with regular hours is congenial to my temperment.							
3. It bothers me when something unexpected interrupts my daily routine.							
4. I don't like to undertake any project unless I have a pretty good idea as to how it will turn out.							
5. I find it hard to set aside a task that I have undertaken, even for a short time.							
6. I don't like things to be uncertain and unpredictable.							

Part II: Organizational Practices

Instructions:

The following statements describe various characteristics of organizational conditions that may or may not exist in your organization. These questions relate to your position in the purchasing department and/or the department itself. For each statement, you are asked to give two (2) ratings.

For column (A): Rate how true is the statement now:

Definitely Not True	1	2	3	4	5	6	7	Extremely True

For Column (B): Rate the desirability of the condition described:

It would be extremely un-desirable if this statement were true.	1	2	3	4	5	6	7	It would be extremely de-sirable if this statement were true.

	Column (A) (Now)	Column (B) (Desirable)
1. Performance appraisals are based on written performance standards or criteria.	1 2 3 4 5 6 7	1 2 3 4 5 6 7
2. Standards of performance and control systems have been published in writing.	1 2 3 4 5 6 7	1 2 3 4 5 6 7
3. Schedules, programs or project specifications are used to guide work.	1 2 3 4 5 6 7	1 2 3 4 5 6 7
4. My duties, authority and accountability are documented in policies, procedures or job descriptions.	1 2 3 4 5 6 7	1 2 3 4 5 6 7
5. Group rules or guidelines to direct efforts are very clear.	1 2 3 4 5 6 7	1 2 3 4 5 6 7
6. Written procedures and guides are available.	1 2 3 4 5 6 7	1 2 3 4 5 6 7
7. The organization works to a written law.	1 2 3 4 5 6 7	1 2 3 4 5 6 7
8. Written documents (such as budgets, schedules, project specifications, procedures, or program plans, job descriptions, etc.) are used as an integral part of the job.	1 2 3 4 5 6 7	1 2 3 4 5 6 7

Part III: Your Immediate Supervisor

Instructions:

The following statements address the relationship that exists between you and your immediate supervisor. For each statement, please circle how true the statement is:

1. He lets group members know what is expected of them.

| Definitely Not True | 1 | 2 | 3 | 4 | 5 | 6 | 7 | Extremely True |

2. He decides what shall be done and how it shall be done.

| Definitely Not True | 1 | 2 | 3 | 4 | 5 | 6 | 7 | Extremely True |

3. He makes sure that his part in the group is understood.

| Definitely Not True | 1 | 2 | 3 | 4 | 5 | 6 | 7 | Extremely True |

4. He schedules the work to be done.

| Definitely Not True | 1 | 2 | 3 | 4 | 5 | 6 | 7 | Extremely True. |

5. He maintains definite standards of performance.

| Definitely Not True | 1 | 2 | 3 | 4 | 5 | 6 | 7 | Extremely True |

6. He asks that group members follow standard rules and regulations.

| Definitely Not True | 1 | 2 | 3 | 4 | 5 | 6 | 7 | Extremely True |

7. He explains the way my tasks should be carried out.

| Definitely Not True | 1 | 2 | 3 | 4 | 5 | 6 | 7 | Extremely True |

Part IV: Your Job

Instructions:

The following statements are questions concerning your job as a purchasing professional. For each statement, please circle how true the statement is:

1. Problems which arise on my job can generally be solved by using standard procedures.

Definitely not   Extremely true
true of my job   1   2   3   4   5   of my job

2. I can generally perform my job by using standardized methods.

Definitely not   Extremely true
true of my job   1   2   3   4   5   of my job

3. Problems which I encounter on my job can generally be solved in a number of different ways.

Definitely not   Extremely true
true of my job   1   2   3   4   5   of my job

4. What is the average time it takes you to complete a typical assignment?

        5 - one day or less
        4 - between 1 and 3 days
        3 - between 3 days and 1 week
        2 - between 1 and 2 weeks
        1 - longer than 2 weeks

5. How repetitious are your duties?

        1 - very little
        2 - some
        3 - quite a bit
        4 - very much
        5 - almost completely

6. How similar are the tasks you perform in a typical work day?

        5 - almost all the same
        4 - quite a few the same
        3 - only a few the same
        2 - very few the same
        1 - almost all different

7. If you were to write a list of activities you would be confronted by on an average work day, what percent of these activities do you think would be interrupted by unexpected events?

           1 - 80 - 100%
           2 - 60 - 80%
           3 - 40 - 60%
           4 - 20 - 40%
           5 - 0 - 20%

8. How much variety is there in the work tasks which you perform?

           1 - very much
           2 - quite a bit
           3 - some
           4 - little
           5 - very little

9. Every job is confronted by certain routine and repetitive demands. What percent of the activities or work demands connected with your job would you consider to be of a routine nature?

           1 - 0 - 20%
           2 - 20 - 40%
           3 - 40 - 60%
           4 - 60 - 80%
           5 - 80 - 100%

10. .The tasks of some individual are more "structured" than others: the goals are clearer, the methods to be used are more understood, and the problems are more repetitive and less unique, for example. Would you please rate what you feel is the degree of "structure" of your job by circling the best response.

My job is highly   My job is highly
   unstructured   1   2   3   4   5   structured

Part V: Self Evaluation of Performance

Instructions:

   Listed below are several dimensions of purchasing positions. Rate yourself in comparison to other purchasers on each dimension by marking the appropriate space on the scale which follows each statement. The numbers and meanings are indicated below:

   If your performance is

           very low   circle number 1
           moderately low   circle number 2
           average   circle number 3
           moderately high   circle number 4
           high   circle number 5

1. Profit Potential - The extent to which your buying activities result in cost savings to your firm.

   low   1   2   3   4   5   high

2. Personal Skills - The successful expenditure of extra effort on your part to convince others in your organization to accept your proposals.

   low   1   2   3   4   5   high

3. Departmental Coordination - Effort you spend in communicating, providing reports, arranging meetings, or providing liaison within your department or organization.

   low   1   2   3   4   5   high

4. Negotiation - The extent to which your discussions with suppliers produce favorable results.

   low   1   2   3   4   5   high

5. Inter-firm Coordination - The extent to which you arrange meetings between yourself, members of your firm, and vendors in order to improve cooperation.

   low   1   2   3   4   5   high

6. Overall Effectiveness - Rate yourself on total performance in your present purchasing position.

   low   1   2   3   4   5   high

Part VI: Description of Purchasing Responsibilities

1. Please check your functional title from the list below:

Vice President of Purchasing: _____	Assistant Purchasing Manager:_____
Director of Purchasing: _____	Assistant Purchasing Agent: _____
Purchasing Manager: _____	Senior Buyer: _____
Purchasing Agent: _____	Buyer: _____

   Other (Please Specify Title):

   _____

2. Please indicate your level of responsibility by checking the appropriate description below:

   Manager/Supervisor, with no direct buying responsibility _____
   Manager/Supervisor, with direct buying responsibility _____
   Buyer, with supervisory responsibility for other buyers _____
   Buyer, with no supervisory responsibility _____
   Other (Please Specify)

   _____

3. What percentage of your time is spent in supervising other purchasing personnel?

0-20%	21-40%	41-60%	61-80%	81-100%

4. Which of the following categories best describes your primary (by dollar volume of purchases) area of buying responsibility?

_____ Metals	_____ Packaging
_____ Electronics	_____ Construction
_____ Mechanical Components	_____ Office Equipment
_____ Chemicals	_____ Services
_____ Capital Equipment	_____ Petroleum Products
_____ MRO	_____ Other _____

(Please Specify)

5. What was the total of the annual purchases made by you in 1984?

_____ (in dollars)

6. Are the purchasing responsibilities in your company (organization) predominantly

_____ centralized
_____ decentralized

7. At what level are your buying responsibilities?

_____ corporate
_____ divisional
_____ plant

Part VII: Your Company and Yourself

Instructions:

Please answer the following questions in the space provided.

1. How large is your company (organization)?

In number of employees   _____
In annual sales (1984 sales)   _____

2. What were the total annual dollars spent on purchases of all products and services by your company (organization) in 1984?   _____

3. Please classify the organization for which you work by checking the appropriate category below:

Industrial
_____ Energy (SIC 10-14)
_____ Construction (SIC 15-17)
_____ Food, tobacco (SIC 20-21)
_____ Textile, leather (SIC 22,23,31)
_____ Lumber (SIC 24)
_____ Furniture (SIC 25)
_____ Paper (SIC 26)
_____ Printing, publishing (SIC 27)
_____ Chemicals (SIC 28)
_____ Petroleum (SIC 29)
_____ Rubber (SIC 30)

_____ Stone, glass, clay (SIC 32)
_____ Primary metals (SIC 32)
_____ Fabricated metals (SIC 34)
_____ Machinery (excluding electrical)(SIC35
_____ Electrical equipment (SIC 36)
_____ Transportation equipment (SIC 37)
_____ Instruments (SIC 38)
_____ Miscellaneous manufacturing (SIC 39)
_____ Transportation (SIC 40-47)
_____ Public Utilities (SIC 48-49)
_____ Service Centers (SIC 50)

Institutional and Other
_____ health related
_____ financial
_____ educational
_____ government

_____ retailing
_____ wholesaler, distributor
_____ business services
_____ R&D, scientific

4. Please answer the following biographical questions:

Age: ☐ 25 or under   Sex: ☐ Male   Educational ☐ High School Graduate
☐ 30 to 40   ☐ Female   Level: ☐ Some College but less than 4 years
☐ 40 to 50   ☐ Bachelor's Degree
☐ 50 and over   ☐ Master's Degree
                                                 ☐ Doctorate

5. How long have you worked for your current company (organization)?

_____

6. How long have you been in your present position?

_____

7. How many years of purchasing experience do you have?

_____

8. Are you a CPM or CPPO? Yes _____ No _____
or other certification (please specify) _____

9. Which of the following categories best describes your current salary?

_____ Less than $20,000	_____ $61,000 to $70,000
_____ $20,000 to $30,000	_____ $71,000 to $80,000
_____ $31,000 to $40,000	_____ $81,000 to $90,000
_____ $41,000 to $50,000	_____ $91,000 to $100,000
_____ $51,000 to $60,000	_____ Over $100,000

Thank you for your participation in this study. If you would like to see a summary of the completed study when it is available, please indicate this by checking the box below and filling in your address. Also, please be assured that your responses will be kept in the strictest confidence and will not be made available to others. Again, thank you for your cooperation.

Michael G. Kolchin
Assistant Professor of Management
College of Business & Economics
Lehigh University
Bethlehem, PA 18015

☐ Yes, I would like a copy of the completed study.

Name _____

Address _____

_____

_____

CENTER FOR ADVANCED PURCHASING STUDIES •

THE CENTER FOR ADVANCED PURCHASING STUDIES (CAPS) was established in November 1986 as an affiliation agreement between the College of Business at Arizona State University and the National Association of Purchasing Management. It is located at The Arizona State University Research Park, 2055 East Centennial Circle, P.O. Box 22160, Tempe, Arizona 85285-2160 (Telephone [602] 752-2277).

The Center has three major goals to be accomplished through its research program:

- to improve purchasing effectiveness and efficiency;
- to improve overall purchasing capability;
- to increase the competitiveness of U.S. companies in a global economy.

Research under way and planned includes Global Purchasing; World-Class Purchasing Organizations and Practices to 1995; Purchasing Benchmarking; Purchasing from Small Women-Owned Suppliers; Purchasing Education and Training Resources and Requirements; the Quality Issue; and Purchasing's Involvement in Transportation Decision-Making.

CAPS, a 501 (c) (3) not-for-profit research organization, is funded solely by tax-deductible contributions from corporations and individuals who want to make a difference in the state of purchasing and materials management knowledge. Policy guidance is provided by the Board of Trustees consisting of:

The Center for Advanced Purchasing Studies and the National Association of Purchasing Management wish to thank the following corporations, foundations, individuals, and affiliated purchasing management associations for their financial support:

CORPORATIONS/FOUNDATIONS

$40,000 and Over
BellSouth Services
Northern Telecom Inc.
US WEST Business Resources, Inc.

$20,000 and Over
ARCO
BP America
Chevron U.S.A. Inc.
Conoco/Du Pont
RJR Nabisco, Inc.
Texas Instruments Incorporated
TRW Foundation
Westinghouse Foundation

$10,000 and Over
AT&T
Carnival Cruise Lines
Caterpillar Inc.
CSX Transportation
Eastman Kodak Company
G.E. Company, Corporate Sourcing
Kraft, Inc.
Lockheed Leadership Fund
Mobil Foundation
Polaroid Corporation
Raytheon Company
Shell Oil Company
Texaco Services, Inc.

Union Pacific Railroad Corporation
UNISYS Corporation

$5,000 and Over
Amoco Corporation
Corning Incorporated
Distribution Magazine—A Chilton
    Company
Exxon Company, U.S.A.
Firestone Trust Fund
The HCA Foundation
Hughes Aircraft
Intel Corporation
NYNEX Materiel Enterprises Company

CORPORATIONS/FOUNDATIONS (continued)

Phillips Petroleum Company
Southern Pacific Transportation Co.
United Technologies Corporation

$4,999 and Under
The American Tobacco Co.
Americhem Inc.
Ameritech Services
ANR Freight Systems, Inc.
Arcop, Inc.
ARGO-TECH Corporation
Avery, Materials Group
Barnes Group Foundation
The Bauer Group
Carter Chemicals & Services, Inc.
C.M. Almy & Sons, Inc.
Coastal Savings Bank
Concord Realstate Corp.
Dragon Products Co.

Ernst & Young
Freeway Corporation
G.E. Company,
  Contracting/Purchasing
The Glidden Company
Haluch & Associates
Imperial Litho/Graphics, Inc.
Industrial Distribution Association
International Minerals &
  Chemicals Corporation
Keithley Instruments, Inc.
The Lincoln Electric Company
Loctite Corporation
L-Tec Welding & Cutting Systems
Marathon Oil Company
N.I.G.P., Arizona State
  Capitol Chapter
North Canton Tool Company
Oatey Company

Ohio Power Company
Olin Corporation
  Charitable Trust
ORYX Energy Company
OXY USA Inc.
Pacific Bell
Parker Hannifin Corporation
Pharmaceutical Manufacturers
  Association
The Quality Castings Co.
Restaurants & Institutions
Reznor
Shamrock Hose & Fitting Company
Simmons Precision Product Inc.
Society Corporation
Union Camp Corporation
The Upjohn Company

AFFILIATED ASSOCIATIONS

Akron
Arizona (Southern)
Arkansas
Bay Area
Boston
Canton
Cinti Demetria
Cleveland
Colorado (Western)
Dallas
Dayton
Delaware
Denver
Detroit
District VI
District VII
District IX
Florida Central
Florida First Coast
Florida Gold Coast
Florida Space Coast

Florida West Coast
Fox Valley, Wisconsin
Georgia
Iowa (Central)
Iowa (Eastern)
Kansas City
Lehigh Valley, Inc.
Lima
Madison Area
Maine
Maryland, Inc.
Memphis
Michigan Assoc. (Southwestern)
Michigan (Western)
Milwaukee
New Jersey
New Mexico
New Orleans, Inc.
Oklahoma City
Old Dominion, Inc. (Virginia)
Oregon

Northeastern PA
Northwestern PA
North Central
Petroleum Industry Buyers Group
Philadelphia Inc.
Pittsburgh, PA
Rhode Island
Sabine-Neches
Spokane
Springfield
St. Louis
Syracuse and Central New York, Inc.
Tennessee (East)
Tenneva
Toledo
Transportation Group
Treasure Valley
Tulsa, Inc.
Twin City
Washington (D.C.)
Youngstown District (Ohio)

INDIVIDUALS

R. Jerry Baker, C.P.M.
William A. Bales, C.P.M.
Diane K. Bishop
Joseph T. Boylan
Robert Breitbart
Patricia G. Cole
Gerard R. Coiley, Sr.
Montague E. Cooper, C.P.M.
Frank Croyl
Walter Eads
Julius Edelmann
Harold E. Fearon, Ph.D., C.P.M.
Ted D. Hadley

John H. Hoagland, Ph.D., C.P.M.
Joan Humphrey, C.P.M.
Richard Lee Jackson, C.P.M.
Robert L. Janson, C.P.M.
Robert Kaminski, C.P.M.
Dr. Kenneth H. Killen
Arnold Lovering, C.P.M.
Frederick W. Ludwig
Walter Mielcarek, C.P.M.
Paul K. Moffat, C.P.M.
Thomas A. Nash, C.P.M.
John P. Negrelli
R.D. Nelson

Robert P. Olson, C.P.M.
Harold F. Puff, Ph.D., C.P.M.
Jon E. Schmiedebusch
Stanley N. Sherman, Ph.D., C.P.M.
Jonathan R. Stegner
Scott Sturzl, C.P.M.
Arthur W. Todd
Dennis Urbonas
Robert F. Weber
Milton Welch
W.A. Westerbeck
Elaine Whittington, C.P.M.
Mr. & Mrs. Harry B. Wiggins